THE PARABLES FOR TODAY

Also Available in the For Today Series:

The Beatitudes for Today by James C. Howell
The Lord's Prayer for Today by William J. Carl III
The Ten Commandments for Today by Walter J. Harrelson

THE PARABLES FOR TODAY

Alyce M. McKenzie

Westminster John Knox Press
LOUISVILLE • LONDON

Book design by Sharon Adams
Cover design by Eric Walljasper, Minneapolis, MN

First edition
Published by Westminster John Knox Press
Louisville, Kentucky

This book is printed on acid-free paper that meets the American National Standards Institute Z39.48 standard. ♾

PRINTED IN THE UNITED STATES OF AMERICA

10 11 12 13 14 15 16 — 10 9 8 7 6 5 4 3

Library of Congress Cataloging-in-Publication Data is on file at the Library of Congress, Washington, D.C.

ISBN-13: 978-0-664-22958-0
ISBN-10: 0-664-22958-1

Contents

Series Introduction

The For Today series is intended to provide reliable and accessible resources for the study of important biblical texts, theological documents, and Christian practices. The series is written by experts who are committed to making the results of their studies available to those with no particular biblical or theological training. The goal is to provide an engaging means to study texts and practices that are familiar to laity in churches. The authors are all committed to the importance of their topics and to communicating the significance of their understandings to a wide audience. The emphasis is not only on what these subjects have meant in the past, but also on their value in the present—"For Today."

Our hope is that the books in this series will find eager readers in churches, particularly in the context of education classes. The authors are educators and pastors who wish to engage church laity in the issues raised by their topics. They seek to provide guidance for learning, for nurture, and for growth in Christian experience.

To enhance the educational usefulness of these volumes, Questions for Discussion are included at the end of each chapter.

We hope the books in this series will be important resources to enhance Christian faith and life.

The Publisher

Introduction

A man was once traveling in Switzerland for the first time, sitting in a train going through the Alps. While he was visually feasting on the towering, white-capped mountains outside his window, the man across from him was reading a detective novel. "How can you read when this is going on outside?" he asked the man. "Wait until you have taken this ride as many times as I have," was the reply.

A wise Bible teacher once told his students, "Many times, when people hear that a familiar text is about to be read, they think to themselves, 'Oh, here we go again.' The fact is that they may never have gone in the first place."

After I had agreed to write this book on the parables of Jesus, I stopped and asked myself, "What were you thinking? You have just agreed to write a book on a subject that already has a mile-long bibliography, much of it produced in the past twenty years. What can you possibly hope to contribute or accomplish?" My answer to myself, after some hard thought, was this: "I am excited about writing this book on the parables of Jesus precisely *because* so many books from varied perspectives have been written recently. I hope to make their key insights available to sharp-thinking people who do not happen to be professional theologians or biblical scholars. I hope to help somebody see, hear, feel, and experience a parable in a way that person has never done before."

Parables are short narrative fictions that seek to make us evaluate our lives. While we think we are interpreting them, they are actually interpreting us! They are a form of oral communication that has appeared in almost every religion and culture. Scholars from a variety of fields are interested in them as forms of oral communication, as literary art, and as expressions of religious and cultural norms. New Testament scholars are interested in them because they are a key means by which Jesus sought to answer the question "What is the reign of God like?" The Jewish people had one answer to that question: God's reign or kingdom would be a time of earthly peace, justice, and freedom from oppression by their enemies ushered in by God's chosen Messiah. The Romans had their answer to the question: Since Caesar is to be worshiped as a god, the reign of God looks like the Roman Empire.

Jesus believed that in his ministry the reign or kingdom or empire of God had been unleashed. The reign of God was present, but not yet fully realized. Where? In his healings and exorcisms, in his table fellowship with those the religious establishment viewed as "unclean," and in his teachings: his parables and his aphorisms.

This book is not an academic exploration of the parables, though such works are immensely helpful and have contributed to this one. This is a book for people who want to reflect on the question "What is the kingdom of God like?" It is probably not a book for everybody, because not everybody cares one way or the other. Despite the fact that Gallup polls regularly tell us that a high percentage of U.S. citizens believe in a personal God, not everybody really wants to think about what daily life would look like if we lived in accordance with God's will. That's too close to home.

One of the things I struggled with when I was trying to decide if I was called to ordained ministry twenty-five years ago was the realization that it was sometimes easier for me to love people in general than particular people. In a similar way, it is easier to talk about God's reign and God's will, and God's love in vague, general terms. We approve of these concepts; we wish them well. In fact, many of us express those well-wishes every week in a worship service when we pray with others, "Thy kingdom come, thy will be done on earth as it is in heaven," in the Lord's Prayer.

But there comes a time in our lives when that weekly mumbling of "thy will be done," "thy kingdom come" fails to satisfy. That Sunday comes when the prayer leaves the pew with us and follows us home, where there are no other voices to drown out our own. The prayer follows us home where it becomes personal and pressing, until, finally, we turn to it and say, "All right! What do you want from me?" Put another way, our question becomes, "How am I to respond to the reign of God?" This book seeks to answer that question by entering into conversation with key parables of Jesus, many of which are as familiar to us as the palm of our own hand. Of course, although we carry those palms around with us, we don't very often study them intently. If you look at yours right now, you will probably see some lines you hadn't noticed before. This book proceeds on the strength of two convictions: that we don't know the parables of Jesus as well as we think, and that their study gives far better directives for our futures than the lines on our palms!

Now that you know my motivation, I'll say something about my method. I am now entering the twenty-fifth year of my ministry as an ordained elder in the United Methodist Church. I served as a pastor for a number of years in Pennsylvania, got a doctoral degree in preaching from Princeton Theological Seminary in the mid-1990s, and for the past several years have been teaching seminary students and pastors the art of preaching, a discipline formally called homiletics, at Perkins School of Theology, Southern Methodist University, in Dallas, Texas. During these years of pastoral and teaching ministries, I have preached on lots of parables and have written several articles and books on Jesus as a wisdom teacher who taught using proverbs and parables. As I have tried to wrap my mind and spirit around the parables, it has occurred to me that Jesus' parables offer four basic answers to the question "What is the kingdom of God like?"

1. The kingdom of God is not under our control.
2. The kingdom of God shows up where we least expect it.
3. The kingdom of God disrupts business as usual.
4. The kingdom of God is a reign of justice and forgiveness.[1]

I confess to being somewhat addicted to alliteration, and I hope it won't annoy the reader too much. But bear with me while I point out that these claims about the kingdom of God call for specific responses. In response to the first claim, we *divest* ourselves of our compulsion to control every aspect of our lives. In response to the second, we ask God to help us *discern* the presence of the kingdom amid the details of daily life. In response to the third, we accept the *disruption* the kingdom brings to our habitual actions and assumptions. In response to the fourth, we set our feet toward the *destination* of God's kingdom of justice and forgiveness that is both yet to be and already within our grasp.

I have organized this study around these four assertions about the kingdom of God. The book has ten chapters, each one making up the material for a session of group study. The first three sessions lay the groundwork for the studies of individual parables that follow. Chapter 1 introduces the purpose of Jesus' parables in light of his understanding of the kingdom of God. Chapter 2 describes the traits or properties that made parables Jesus' favorite teaching tool. Chapter 3 explores the different soils in which the evangelists Matthew, Mark, and Luke planted the parables, the contexts in which they placed Jesus' parables to address the needs of those to whom they wrote.[2]

The rest of the chapters (4–10) explore specific parables from Matthew, Mark, and Luke in light of our four claims about the reign of God. We shall see that the parables of the Gospel of Mark offer an "Amen!" to the first statement about the kingdom of God (it is not under our control), whereas Matthew and Luke, each in their own way, applaud the last three affirmations regarding the discernment, disruption, and destination of the kingdom of God (it shows up where we least expect it; it disrupts business as usual; and it leads to justice and forgiveness).

No organizational scheme can do justice to the scope and richness of the parables. Nor is there space, in one brief study, to deal with every single parable. So here, at the very beginning, I invite you to be on the lookout for themes or details you think are important that I neglect, and for places where you want to nuance or disagree with my portrayal of a parable's purpose or theme. Your responses can spark discussion with others, which is, as we shall see, a primary reason Jesus chose parables to point to the reign of God in our midst.

What Parables Do

A parable is a short narrative fiction that expresses a moral or religious lesson. It is a cousin to the proverb, which, as Miguel de Cervantes once said, is a "short sentence founded upon long experience."[3] Parables and proverbs are forms of communication used to convey wisdom and practical strategies for daily living. They are found in almost every religion and culture as a form of oral communication that is subsequently recorded for later generations.

These two oral forms of wisdom teaching, parables and proverbs, have in common the dynamic of drawing lessons from patterns observed in daily life and using vivid imagery to connect with listeners. Both forms seek to involve listeners, to put us to work figuring out how they apply to various situations in our daily lives.

Parables, found in a variety of religious traditions, are often reported as having been uttered by the religion's founder. Like proverbs, they express aspects of the worldview of a particular religion and offer guidance to individuals wishing to become disciples. A Buddhist parable, for example, compares the practice of the Way with a zither, whose strings need to be just the right tightness. Too much practice makes the person tense (strings too tight) and not enough makes a person lazy (strings too loose).[4]

Contemporary Parables

Theologians, philosophers, and novelists have used parables to encourage readers to reflect on their assumptions and their life experiences. Philosopher and theologian Søren Kierkegaard (1813–55) composed parables to encourage readers to reflect on and grow from their life experiences.[5] Lebanese philosopher, artist, and poet Kahlil Gibran (1883–1931) expressed his insights in parables, most famously in the volume *The Madman: His Parables and Poems* (1918). Novelist Franz Kafka (1883–1924), through his parables, expressed his experience of the estrangement and isolation of humans from one another and the divine. One of Kafka's most famous parables is a story called "An Imperial Message," in which a message from a dying emperor represents his own impossible quest for knowledge.[6] Twentieth-century parabolists include Argentinian novelist Jorge Luis Borges (1899–1986), Italian novelist and short-story writer Italo Calvino (1923–85), and Israeli novelist S. Y. Agnon (1888–1970).

Old Testament Parables

As wisdom genres in the Hebrew Scriptures, both proverbs and parables come under the heading of the wisdom genre called a *mashal.* A genre is an oral or literary form of communication that has a certain text, texture, and context. A parable, for example, as a *text*, whether oral or written, is a brief narrative. A parable's *texture,* or internal characteristics, involves portrayals of images, characters, and scenes drawn from the daily life of listeners or readers. The *context* in which parables are spoken or written varies. Within varied settings, the parable's purpose may be to teach a moral lesson, to offer an interpretation of a traditional teaching or text, or, sometimes, as in Jesus' parables, to startle listeners out of settled habits of thinking and acting.

So, what about the genre *mashal,* to which the parable belongs? The noun *mashal* comes from the root (*m-sh-l*) which means "to be like."[7] The term is used in the Old Testament to refer to a number of literary forms that arise from the close observation of daily life and are characterized by vivid, evocative language. They include proverbs, similes, riddles, and brief narratives. Proverbs are far more prevalent in the Old Testament than parables. Two clear examples of parables in the Old Testament are Ezekiel's tale of the eagles (Ezek. 17:3–10) and Nathan's warning to David (2 Sam. 12:1–6).

Rabbinic Parables

The teachers of Judaism from the second through fourth centuries CE used parables a great deal. They are part of what the Jewish tradition calls "midrash," a body of writings that explain existing scriptural texts. "Midrash" is used, not just to refer to the writings themselves, but also to the method of interpretation used in those writings. That method is to use brief narratives to illuminate how a scriptural text written in the past should be interpreted in current daily life. They are often told to illuminate a single verse in Scripture. Like Jesus' parables, they focus on the action of a main character and describe a general situation, not a specific past event. Unlike Jesus' parables, they do not normally involve elements of paradox or the strategy of exaggeration, often referred to as hyperbole, as Jesus' parables often do.

Here is a rabbinic parable told by Rabbi Simeon ben Yohai as a midrash (explanation) on Leviticus 4:6. The parable makes the general point that many may suffer because of one.

Rabbi Simeon ben Yohai taught: A parable. It is like men who were sitting in a ship. One took a drill and began boring beneath his own place. His fellow travelers said to him: "What are you doing?" He said to them: "What does that matter to you? Am I not drilling under my own place?" They said: "Because the water will come up and flood the ship for us all."[8]

The rabbis' use of parables continued through the medieval Jewish philosophers, the best known of whom was Moses Maimonides. Jewish mysticism as it developed in Spain in the thirteenth century (*Qabbalah*) and Eastern European rabbinic teachings of the eighteenth and nineteenth centuries also used parables.

Jesus' Parables

In the study that follows we will focus on Jesus' parables as recounted in Matthew, Mark, and Luke. These three Gospels have much material in common. They depict Jesus as one who taught in short proverbial sayings (aphorisms) and in parables. They depict his teachings as focused on answering two questions: "What is the kingdom of God like?" and, "How should we live so that we participate in it, both now and in the future?" Taken together, the Gospels of Matthew, Mark, and Luke contain over 102 proverbial sayings and 40 parables.[9] Because of the similarities among them, these three Gospels are usually called the Synoptic Gospels (from the Greek word *synopsis*, a "seeing together"). John's Gospel, by contrast, refers to the kingdom of God only once (John 3:5). Jesus' teachings take the form of a series of explanations of his identity and mission that are often called the "I am" sayings.[10] While John features several shorter, proverblike sayings of Jesus, it includes none of the short narrative parables we encounter in the other three Gospels.

One of the books I have on my shelves is called *Gospel Parallels*, a book that sets forth the text of the three Synoptic Gospels (Matthew, Mark, and Luke) in parallel columns.[11] Thumbing through this book, you can't help noticing that there is a great deal of content these three Gospels have in common.[12]

It is obvious that there is some sort of literary relationship among these three Gospels. The explanation most biblical scholars today accept is the theory that Mark was written first (around 70 CE) and that Matthew (85–90 CE) and Luke (90–95 CE) borrowed the Gospel of Mark's historical narrative, but arranged its material to suit their own purpose in writing for their communities.

Mark was not the only source used by Matthew and Luke. If we spend a little more time thumbing through the *Gospel Parallels*, we will notice that there is a body of material that is common to Matthew and Luke that does not appear in Mark. A number of biblical scholars have theorized that this material comes from another source, one that was used by both Matthew and Luke but not by Mark. They call this the Q source (for *Quelle*, the German word for "source").[13] It may have developed in an early itinerant movement of Christians seeking, as a community, to live by Jesus' ethical teachings.

Suppose that you become so intrigued by the *Gospel Parallels* that you decide to send your family away on vacation for two weeks so you can stay behind, home alone, poring over the Gospel parallels, barely able to tear yourself away to eat and sleep. As you sit in your chair, hunched over the volume, you discover that Q is not the only source that Matthew and Luke used in addition to Mark. There is also some material in each Gospel, Matthew and Luke, including some parables, that is unique to each of them. You would find that there are about 300 verses in Matthew and 520 in Luke that have no parallel in any of the other Gospels.[14] In Luke most of them come in the section between Luke 9:51 and 18:14. It contains many distinctive parables of Jesus, such as those of the Good Samaritan, the Rich Fool, the Lost Coin,the Lost Sheep, the Prodigal Son, the Dishonest Steward, the Unjust Judge, and the Pharisee and the Tax Collector.[15]

1

The Purpose of Jesus' Parables

Jesus uses the wisdom forms of proverb and parable for a different purpose than the sages of the Old Testament or the later rabbis. They used them to reinforce conventional wisdom. Read a couple of chapters of Proverbs and you'll see that the sages were giving the kind of advice parents still give their teenagers. Their sayings promote moderation, hard work, and restraint in one's speech as the path to security and longevity. "The highway of the upright avoids evil; those who guard their way preserve their lives" (Prov. 16:17). Jesus, by contrast, uses the proverbial form to challenge security as a goal for living and to encourage radical reliance on God. A primary way he does this is by using paradox. "Those who want to save their life will lose it, and those who lose their life . . . will save it" (Mark 8:35; Luke 17:33; Matt. 10:39; John 12:25).

A clear example of Jesus' subversive use of proverbial saying is in his Beatitudes. In the Old Testament, beatitudes describe blessings that come in ways we would expect: from obeying God, helping the poor, or studying Torah (Ps. 1:1–2). One who engages in these practices is surrounded by a sphere of well-being and divine favor. Jesus describes states of blessedness that come in ways we would not normally expect: from being poor, mourning, being persecuted, and being hungry and thirsty.

What is true for Jesus' use of proverbs is true for his use of parables. Jesus uses parables to subvert traditional wisdom and to point to a new, inbreaking reality, the kingdom of God. He places seemingly everyday stories next to this new reality, the reign or kingdom of God, and allows the connections and the disconnections between the two to spark in the hearer's mind.[1] This is very different from the rabbis' use of parables to illustrate a traditional interpretation of individual verses of the Torah. Jesus' use of parables is summed up in the phrase that we find several times in the Sermon on the Mount (Matt. 5–7): "You have heard it said . . . but I say to you. . . ."

The expression "the kingdom of God" occurs nowhere in the Old Testament or in the Apocrypha, books written between the Old and New Testaments that are accepted as part of the canon by the Roman Catholics but not by Protestants. The idea of the kingship of God is pervasive in the Old Testament, appearing in the historical narratives (Exod. 15:18; 2 Kgs. 19:15), the Psalms (Pss. 29:10; 103:19), and the Prophets (Isa. 43:15). The concept of God's kingship has both a present and a future aspect. God is already king, having made the world and now governing it in righteousness. At the same time, God's kingship lies in the future. God is the one true God, whose will must prevail, but as yet he is known only to his people. His people look for a coming day when God will overcome all competing forces and establish himself as King of Kings.[2] In the meantime they seek to live in obedience to God, hoping thereby to hasten God's intervention.

In Israel's history, the king, in ruling the land, was to embody the attributes of God. His duty was to act out of concern for justice for the poor. After Israel no longer had historical kings, this job description was transferred to the messianic king, or the saving figure who would usher in the new order of God. This leader would restore justice to the land and participate in judgment, a royal function.[3]

By Jesus' time some Jews expected the restoration of the nation under Davidic rule and the end of Roman rule. Others expected a dramatic intervention by God in which a supernatural saving figure would inaugurate a kingdom that would encompass the entire world, with Jerusalem the Holy City and the Temple at its center. Some groups hoped for both at the same time. The burning question for every Jew in the first century was "What must I do to enter this kingdom when it comes?"[4]

Several groups within first-century Judaism offered varying answers to this question. The Sadducees, the priestly aristocracy, had this answer: Let's preserve our national identity as the people of God by preserving the Temple, and let's safeguard Jerusalem by collaborating with the Romans.

The Essenes were a separatist group. Their best-known community was the colony at Qumran near the Dead Sea. They had this answer to the question "What shall we do to enter the kingdom?" Let's establish separate communes in towns and cities throughout the country, hold everything in common, employ very precise rituals of purification, engage in farm labor, and interpret Torah very strictly.

The Zealots had this answer: Let's gather the poor of the rural areas, who are impoverished by high Roman and Temple taxes. Let's train with them for military rebellion to liberate Jerusalem from Roman occupation.

The Pharisees had still another answer to the question "What shall we do to enter the kingdom of God?" Let's not separate from the people, but let's seek to be a "holy people of priests" in the midst of everyday life. Let's observe the dietary laws given to us in the Torah to keep us holy and pure, to preserve our identity as a people. Since the observance of the Sabbath has long been a key symbol of our election by God, let's keep the Sabbath with great precision. Let's form groups in the towns where we live and eat together in rigorous cleanliness, in keeping with the Levitical laws.[5]

It is not fair to caricature the Pharisees, as has much Christian scholarship, as legalistic adherents to a religion of works righteousness. Judaism, both of Jesus' day and today, is a religion of a gracious and faithful God who initiates the covenant relationship with Israel. The Pharisees of the first century saw following the commandments as a way of saying "Yes" to God's prior gracious outreach to the nation. It was a way of maintaining her identity in the midst of Gentile oppression and defilement, a Roman occupation characterized by idolatry, exploitation, and violence.[6]

Jesus' interpretation of Israel's identity focused, not on the holiness of the elect, but on the wholeness of the people. His ministry was directed to the destitute, the sick, and the crippled, tax collectors, sinners, and prostitutes. Gentiles as well as Jews were included in his table fellowship. His ministry encompassed women as well as men. His parables take their images from the world of women, looking for coins, beseeching unjust judges, and baking bread. His healings and exorcisms make women whole.[7] Jesus and his movement did not observe the purity regulations and even shared meals with "sinners." Jesus' central image of the kingdom is not the cultic meal, but the royal banquet or wedding feast. This difference was probably one of the major conflicts between the movement that arose out of Jesus' ministry and the Pharisaic movement.

We can see by this brief description of Jewish renewal groups in Jesus' time that, though they differed in what course of action was needed to enter the kingdom of God, they shared the expectation of its imminent arrival. The Kaddish, a prayer used in Jewish synagogues in the first century, expressed the hope for God's immediate intervention.

> Magnified and sanctified be his great name
> In the world that he has created according to his will.
> May he establish his kingdom in your lifetime and in your day
> And in the lifetime of all the house of Israel,
> Even speedily and at a near time.[8]

The Proclamation of Jesus' Parables

The Reign: What Is the Kingdom of God Like?

The future of the kingdom was the time when justice and peace would be established, when the nation would be saved, evil would be defeated, and YHWH himself would rule in justice and peace. So Jesus instructs his disciples to pray, "Your kingdom come" (Matt. 6:10; Luke 11:2). Jesus' notion of the kingdom shared this "not yet" quality of Jewish expectation. (See Matt. 8:11; 20:21; Mark 9:1). He also portrayed the kingdom of God as a reality that is already present in his teachings, healings, and exorcisms. God's gracious initiative to us makes the kingdom possible. Our human response is a necessary ingredient in its coming into being.

Jesus' claim that the kingdom was present in his teachings, healings, and exorcisms was shocking because it so strongly implied his divine identity. Where the leader, God's chosen one, was present, the kingdom was already present. The presence of the kingdom meant that God's anointed Messiah was here and was at work—that he was, in fact, accomplishing the sovereign and saving rule of God.[9]

The term "kingdom of God" in Jesus' teaching does not refer to a territory or a geographical domain. It does not refer to a utopian social order that would be established by human efforts on earth. It is not to be equated with any political philosophy or agenda. It suggests the idea of a "reign," highlighting the relationship between the sovereign God and the individual. Says New Testament scholar Bruce Metzger, "Jesus urged his hearers to recognize God's sovereignty as a present reality, to be acknowledged by a personal response, . . . and he also led them to hope for a new age in which human hardness of heart would no longer prevent God's sovereignty from finding universal and complete response."[10]

The Gospels depict the kingdom as something near at hand, into which people can enter (Mark 1:15). It is given as a gift (Luke 12:32). It is not a national or racial privilege (Matt. 8:12; 21:43). The condition for entry into the kingdom is doing God's will (Matt. 7:21–23). Before one can do God's will, one must repent and be converted, completely changing one's priorities and perspective (Matt. 4:17; Mark 1:15). The kingdom must be a person's first priority (Matt. 6:33; Luke 12:31), for which one is prepared to give up everything else (Matt. 13:44–46). While the initiative in establishing the relationship with the individual belongs to God, the responsibility for responding to that initiative belongs to us (Luke 12:31–32; Matt. 7:21). The kingdom will manifest itself in the future (Mark 9:1), when the Son of Man comes with his angels in the glory of his Father (Matt. 16:27). This kingdom, appointed by the Father to Jesus, is to be enjoyed by those who Jesus determines are worthy to share its joys (Luke 22:25–29).[11]

The Ruler: What Is God Like?

The parables imply, rather than directly state, an answer to the question "What is God like?" For one thing, God is sovereign, sowing his word in whatever soil he chooses (Sower: Mark 4:3–8). God is forgiving and expects the same from us (Unforgiving Servant: Matt. 18:23–34). God takes great pains not to destroy evil where good might be destroyed as well (Weeds among the Wheat: Matt. 13:24–30). God gives generously to those who ask of him (Friend at Midnight: Luke 11:5–8). God is gracious and merciful beyond all expectation and does not reward solely on the basis of merit (Workers in the Vineyard: Matt.

20:1–16). God goes to great lengths to save the lost, especially those shamed by the larger society (Lost Sheep, Lost Coin, and Lost Son: Luke 15). God entrusts all people with the task of investing their lives, their time and abilities—in the kingdom (Talents: Matt. 25:14–30). God holds us accountable for our actions (Dishonest Steward: Luke 16:1–13; Fishnet: Matt. 13:47–50; Faithful and Unfaithful Servants: Matt. 24:45–51; Luke 12:42–46).[12] In short, the God of the parables is a God who demands all, but who, at the same time, gives all.

Jesus' Identity

Jesus taught directly about the kingdom of God in the Synoptic Gospels, not as directly about himself. He left it largely up to his disciples to infer his identity from his teachings and actions. Those who observed and experienced Jesus used three existing categories to describe his identity: Messiah, Son of Man, and Son of God. We get a glimpse into Jesus' expression of the Divine in the way he accepted, rejected, and adapted each of these traditional expectations.

Messiah

The title "Messiah" is a Hebrew word meaning "anointed" (Greek= *Christos*; English=Christ). The term was used in the Old Testament to refer to those anointed with oil for a special function such as that of the high priest (Lev. 4:3, 5, 16) or the king (2 Sam. 1:14, 16). During the late Old Testament period (400–300 BCE), the title "Messiah" came to denote the ideal king anointed by God, empowered by God's spirit to deliver his people and establish his kingdom in righteousness (Dan. 9:26–27). Jesus seems to have been reluctant to apply the title to himself due to its political, nationalistic overtones. When others directly confronted him with a statement of his messiahship, he did not deny it (Matt. 16:15–17; Mark 8:29–30; 14:61–62).

The Son of Man

Instead of using the term "Messiah," Jesus preferred to refer to himself as the "Son of Man." This term always comes from the lips of Jesus himself, never from his disciples, followers, petitioners, or adversaries.[13] The title had gathered to itself a variety of meanings by Jesus' time. In the book of Ezekiel it meant a human being in general, emphasizing the frailty of a human in the sight of Almighty God. In Ezekiel, where it occurs more than ninety times, it is rendered in the NRSV as "mortal."

In the book of Daniel, "son of man" stood for a figure that both represented the saints of the Most High and had been chosen by God to rule over them. The book of Daniel refers to "one like a human being," or literally, "like a son of man," who stands before God representing the saints of the Most High, and is given "dominion and glory and kingship" (Dan. 7:13–14).

In the later apocalyptic books of *The Similitudes of Enoch* (chaps. 37–61) and *2 Esdras* (chap. 13), the Son of Man has become a superhuman being, the Elect One, who will appear as the messianic ruler of the kingdom of God.

So by Jesus' time the title "Son of Man" had the following connotations: representative human being, holy designated ruler, and future, supernatural messianic figure. Jesus modified and enlarged these traditional meanings in several of his teachings. He asserts that the Son of Man must suffer, die, and be resurrected (Matt. 20:18, 28; 26:45; Mark 8:31; 10:33; 14:21, 41; Luke 18:31; 19:10).

Jesus identifies the Son of Man with the suffering servant of the Lord depicted by the prophet Isaiah (Isa. 53:10–12; Mark 10:45). The Suffering Servant in Isaiah is an unnamed, mysterious figure whose suffering would be redemptive for Israel. In identifying the Son of Man with the Suffering Servant, Jesus combines the motifs of humiliation, suffering, and death with that of the future exaltation of the Son of Man. Clearly he preferred to apply to himself an ambiguous term which he could define more precisely to express the mystery of his identity and mission. The use of the term Son of Man on Jesus' lips is a paradox. It expresses Jesus' solidarity with human beings, yet it distinguishes him from us. It connects him both with earthly humiliation and with coming glory.[14]

Son of God

We've looked at the title "Messiah," which was applied to Jesus by others and at the title "Son of Man," which Jesus applied to himself. A third title, "Son of God," comes from both sides. The title is applied to him by others with his approval (Matt. 16:16; Mark 3:11; 5:7; 14:61; Luke 8:28). Jesus also speaks of himself as "the Son" and calls

God his Father in a direct, familiar way. In Matthew 11:27 (and Luke 10:22), Jesus speaks of his unique relationship of Sonship to the Father. He assumes the title in his claiming of authority to forgive sin (Mark 2:5–7; Luke 5:21) and in his requirement of total commitment of his followers to himself (Matt. 10:32; 10:37; Luke 14:26–27). The implied and overt claim of Sonship contributed heavily to "the inveterate acrimony and hostility that pursued him to his death."[15]

The Response: What Is Discipleship Like?

What do the parables tell us about how we need to respond to God if we seek to participate in God's kingdom? Those who want to follow Christ must be prepared to abandon whatever might stand in the way of wholehearted discipleship (Treasure Hidden in Field: Matt. 13:44; the Pearl of Great Price: Matt. 13:45–46). They acknowledge their unworthiness to earn God's favor (Pharisee and Publican: Luke 18:10–14a). They commit themselves to investing their time and abilities for God's kingdom (parable of the Talents: Matt. 25:14–30; parable of the Pounds: Luke 19:12–24) and to making concern for society's oppressed and afflicted a priority (Good Samaritan: Luke 10:25–37; Rich Man and Lazarus: Luke 16:19–31). They avoid the idolatry that comes with the needless accumulation of possessions (Rich Farmer: Luke 12:16–20; Unforgiving Servant: Matt. 18:23–34). They do not presume to know how long they have to participate in the kingdom on earth. They remain alert to the possibility that the end could come at any moment (Returning Master: Mark 13:34–36; Ten Bridesmaids: Matt. 25:1–13).[16]

They bring their needs to God in prayer, boldly and without shame (Friend at Midnight: Luke 11:5–8; Widow and Unjust Judge: Luke 18:2–5). They look forward to seeing the kingdom grow into a powerful force despite its inauspicious beginning and often imperceptible presence (Mark 4:1–34 and parallels). They do not begrudge God's generosity to others (Prodigal Son: Luke 15:11–32). They realize the consequences of disobedience and faithlessness (Two Sons: Matt. 21:28–32; Wicked Tenants: Mark 12:1–9; Matt. 21:33–39; Luke 20:9–15a; Great Feast: Luke 14:16–24; Matt. 22:1–14). Those who persevere to the end will ultimately be rewarded with eternal fellowship with God and the company of all believers (Weeds among the Wheat: Matt. 13:24–30; Fishnet: Matt. 13:47–50; Rich Man and Lazarus: Luke 16:19–31; Faithful and Unfaithful Servants: Matt. 24:45–51; Luke 12:42–48).[17]

Now that we have had this brief overview of the understanding of the kingdom of God in the Synoptic Gospels, the question arises, "How can we notice the kingdom amid all the noise of daily life?" Here is a hint. We are looking and listening and watching for something that is not under our control, that shows up when and where we least expect it, that disrupts business as usual, and that leads to justice and forgiveness.

We shall explore the various visions of the kingdom of God in Mark, Matthew, and Luke in chapter 3. Before we do that, we need to ask the question "What are the properties of parables that make them so well suited to convey Jesus' vision of the kingdom of God?" That will be our focus in chapter 2.

Questions for Discussion

1. How do you interpret the statement that God gives all and demands all? How is this challenging? How is this comforting or inspiring?
2. How does Jesus' use of parables differ from that of the rabbis?
3. What do you think is commendable in the intentions of the Pharisees? What may have led to some superficial practices of the faith? In what ways are we in the same danger today?

2

The Properties of Jesus' Parables

Parables and proverbs are members of a family of literature called *mashal* ("to be like") in Hebrew, and *parabole* ("to set alongside") in Greek. The term *mashal* in the Old Testament is used to refer to a diverse group of communication forms: a proverb, a taunt, a riddle, a story parable, or even an allegory. These forms contain concrete images and events, arising from the close observation of daily life, with the purpose of causing listeners or readers to reflect on situations in their own lives in light of the *mashal*.

Since the parables are Jesus' answer to the question "What is the kingdom of God like?" it's accurate to say that the parables of Jesus are comparisons. Some of his parables are brief similes. We remember from schooldays that a simile is an explicit comparison introduced by "like" or "as." For example, "The kingdom of God is like treasure hidden in a field . . . a merchant in search of fine pearls, . . . a net thrown into the sea" (Matt. 13:44–50). The kingdom of God is like a grain of mustard seed (Mark 4:30–32). It is "like yeast that a woman took and hid . . ." (Matt. 13:33).

What about Jesus' longer, narrative parables? How are we to understand the way they use comparison to help us answer the question "What is the kingdom of God like?" The traditional view, from the time of the early church fathers until the late 1800s, was that the parables are allegories. An allegory is a story in which every character, event, and image stands for something else beyond the story itself. By this view, each feature of the parable actually refers to a reality outside the story.

A clear example of an allegory is *The Pilgrim's Progress,* an allegorical novel by John Bunyan published in 1678. The main character, Christian, journeys from the City of Destruction to the Celestial City, with stop-offs at places like the Slough of Despond and the hill Difficulty, meeting characters such as Faithful and Mr. Worldly Wiseman. It is crystal clear, in this intentional allegory, how each character, town, and event stands for an aspect of the journey of salvation. Compare this with the sermon I once heard based on an allegorical interpretation of the Good Samaritan. For the preacher, the parable was an allegorical account of salvation history. The man was traveling from Jerusalem (salvation) to Jericho (destruction). The Good Samaritan (Jesus) anointed the man's wounds with wine (Jesus' blood for our salvation) and oil (Jesus' royal authority), thus reversing the journey from destruction back to salvation.

Between Jesus' death around 30 CE and the writing of the Gospel of Mark (around 70 CE), Jesus' parables were told and retold by people, with added details according to the context in which the parable was being recounted. It seems clear that first-century interpreters of Jesus' parables used allegory to connect features of his parables with their own political, religious, and congregational contexts. Several of the parables seem to have allegorical explanations attached to them. Mark 4:13–20, for example, is an allegorical interpretation of the parable of the Sower in Mark 4:3–9. It seems to be directed toward an early church community facing temptations to fall away from faith in Jesus because of persecution or seduction by wealth. Christians here are applying the details of a parable about farming in rural Palestine to church life in the latter half of the first century.[1]

Matthew 13:36–43 is an allegorical explanation of the parable of the Weeds among the Wheat in Matthew 13:24–30. It contains the theme of judgment emphasized in Matthew's Gospel as well as the uniquely Matthean phrase, "weeping and gnashing of teeth."

Mark 12:1–11, the parable of the Wicked Tenants, certainly seems to be a clear-cut allegory of the sending of prophets, culminating in the sending of Jesus, and their rejection by Israel. A version of this parable in a collection of Jesus' sayings called the *Gospel of Thomas* omits the conclusion we find in Mark (12:9–11), in which the owner comes and destroys the tenants and gives the vineyard to others. The parable in *Thomas* leaves it up to the reader to answer the question that is explicit in Mark's version: "What then will the vineyard owner do?"(Mark 12:9a).[2]

Allegorical interpretations of Jesus' parables in the Synoptic Gospels often bear the fingerprints of early church communities. Matthew is more prone to allegory than Luke, whose parables focus more on human emotion in realistic situations (Prodigal Son; Good Samaritan). Matthew tends to end the parables that are unique to his Gospel with someone being judged and rejected or sent away (Planted Weeds, Unmerciful Servant, Vineyard Laborers, Last Judgment). Often he has in mind the Pharisees, leaders of a movement in Judaism that came into their own in the late first century CE. The movement was present in Jesus' time, but by the time of the writing of Matthew (around 85–90 CE), their influence had increased. Many scholars feel that Matthew enhances the frequency and bitterness of Jesus' attacks on them in his Gospel. The reason seems to be that his community, near the end of the first century, was locked in conflict with members of the Pharisees who were leaders of the local synagogue(s). We need to remember that there were Pharisees who did follow Jesus. It is also important to point out that the equation of Pharisee with narrow-mindedness, works righteousness, and legalism is not fair to the intentions or the integrity of many in the movement in Jesus' day. Contemporary Christian readers need to be very careful not to interpret the parables in anti-Semitic ways, connecting the villains and the judged in the parables with the Jews and those who are righteous or approved with Christians.

Parables scholar Robert Stein rightly advises us as contemporary readers of Jesus' parables that "We should find allegory in the parables of Jesus only when we must, not simply when we can!"[3] This is a good guideline to allow the challenge of the parables to speak to us in places where we need to accept judgment for our actions. Some biblical interpreters encourage readers to make a habit of identifying with the least appealing characters in a parable. This is a good way to make sure that we are not avoiding our own faults and injustices.

I would like to think of myself as a sheep, not a goat, as a forgiving person, someone others can count on for help, someone who uses my resources to help the poor, a tree bearing good fruit, someone who, when I see someone lying by the road, stops and helps without hesitation. But maybe I need to ask myself if sometimes and in some ways I am a goat, a weed, an unforgiving servant, an unjust judge, a wealthy person who steps over Lazarus lying on my front step, a barren tree, or a person crossing the road to avoid contact with someone lying in a ditch.

German scholar Adolf Jülicher, writing in the late 1880s, pointed out that parables are not best understood as allegories, but rather as comparisons between scenes from village life and the kingdom of God. While that was a helpful insight, he then went on to insist that every parable boiled down to a single moral lesson that sounds like a one-liner you would read in a fortune cookie. The parable of the Unjust Steward, in his view, taught that "determined use of the present is a prerequisite for a happy future." The parable of the Talents taught that "Reward is only earned by performance."[4]

The trouble with both ways of interpreting parables—allegory and moral lessons—is that they ignore the historical setting of the parables. Biblical scholar C. H. Dodd in the 1930s and '40s emphasized that Jesus was not talking to twentieth-century people, but to first-century people. He insisted that the issues and controversies of Jesus' day were a crucial context for understanding his parables. He asked the question "If Jesus' parables were just bland moral lessons, how can we explain the hostile reaction to them?" Hostility makes sense, however, if the parables were pointed challenges to the attitudes and actions of his audience and a powerful defense of his own.[5]

Two insights that will shape our discussion of individual parables are that the evangelists were theologians with unique agendas and that the parables are vignettes that serve the purpose of social criticism. New Testament scholar Joachim Jeremias, in his *Parables of Jesus*, first published in 1954, built on Dodd's work, emphasizing that the theological agendas of the evangelists affected how they understood the parables and where they placed them in their Gospels. Their pre-parable setups and post-parable interpretations often differ. For example, Matthew places the parable of the Lost Sheep (Matt. 18:12–13) in the context of how to treat members of the community who have strayed. Luke places it in the context of three parables in chapter 15 that offer metaphors for God's seeking and saving the lost (Luke 15:4–6).

Another insight into parables has been spotlighted by scholars over the past twenty years or so. It is that they are not just abstract pieces of theological reflection, but scenarios that contain concrete social critique of the political and religious powers of Jesus' day.

Biblical scholar C. H. Dodd's definition of a parable, dating back to 1935, still is the best attempt to list the properties of Jesus' parables. We shall see these properties at work in later chapters as we explore individual parables. He defined a parable as "a metaphor or simile drawn from nature or common life, arresting the hearer by its vividness or strangeness, and leaving the mind in sufficient doubt about its precise application to tease it into active thought."[6] Dodd's definition applies several adjectives to Jesus' parables, which we'll now explore. They are realistic, yet strange, paradoxical, metaphorical, challenging, and open-ended. His list of adjectives related to parables reminds me of the old rhyme about bridal attire: "Something old, something new, something borrowed, something blue." Normally, I stick to prose, where I belong, but if I were composing a poem for parables it would describe them as having "something realistic, something strange, something within view, and something out of range."

Realistic, Yet Strange

Parables are realistic, in that they draw on aspects of daily village life in the first century. The familiarity of the images tells us that the kingdom is near, within the realm of our daily experience. Along with their realistic, or familiar, elements, they also feature something strange. That is, they contain some oddity or exaggeration that somehow exceeds or even contradicts the normal daily experience of their hearers or readers. A ridiculously large harvest results from scattered grain (Sower, Mark 4:8). A servant owes a king an amount that could not be paid off in several lifetimes (Unmerciful Servant, Matt. 18:23–34).

I was once teaching a Sunday school class on the parables in a local church. The members were mostly couples in their forties and fifties. I began by saying, "The parables seem like ordinary stories from first-century Palestinian village life. They seem realistic. But then, as we get into them, there is something strange, something not true to life as we know it, something out of whack, off-kilter. Can you think of something in your experience that is realistic and yet strange? One of the women raised her hand. "I'm Alma, and this is my husband, Ken. I am realistic, and Ken is strange!" Good for a laugh, but a concept worth remembering when we come to study individual parables. I think of the gap between what is realistic and what is strange in a parable as a window cracked open just a bit. Through that opening we can look out at what the landscape of life would look like if we, singly and together, lived in God's kingdom. Through it we can also, standing outside, look in on our lives and glimpse a troubling contrast between what we are and do and what is God's will for us and our communities. Wherever we stand with regard to this open window, a parable gives the gift of a glimpse of the kingdom of God, which is present in our experience but operates by values and with results that seem strange to us.

Paradoxical

So much for the adjectives "realistic" and "strange." What about "paradoxical"? A paradox operates by equating opposites and teasing our minds into figuring out how they could possibly be identified with one another. For example, in observing the life of someone else, we might conclude, "Her talent is her curse," or "His affliction is a blessing." What is strange about a parable is precisely this paradoxical equation. It equates something we normally think of as negative with something that, with regard to God's kingdom, is positive. Someone looked down on and despised is the one who acts like a neighbor (Luke 10:30–35); a wily steward's dubious business practices are commended to those who would enter the kingdom of God (Luke 16:8a); an employer's paying workers who work for one hour the same as those who have worked all day is portrayed as a good thing rather than as horribly unfair (Matt 20:1–15).

Metaphorical

Several of Jesus' narrative parables are metaphors in story form that equate a scene from first-century Palestinian life, but with a strange, unrealistic feature, to the kingdom of God. If a simile is an explicit, specific comparison between two like things joined by "like" or "as," a metaphor is an equation of two things not conventionally seen as alike. For example, "Life is an obstacle course," or Paul's reference to his unnamed affliction as a "thorn in the flesh" (2 Cor. 12:7). Metaphorical equation is not literal, but is meant to cause likenesses and unlikenesses to spark back and forth between the two things being equated so that fresh insights into both are created. This is often what I believe Jesus was doing when he placed his short narratives next to the mysterious notion of the kingdom of God. He was giving listeners the chance to reflect on how the kingdom is like and unlike our everyday existence, how it occurs in the midst of our everyday pursuits, yet, at the same time, challenges those pursuits.

Challenging

The list of adjectives we have applied to Jesus' parables so far is that they are realistic, strange, paradoxical, and metaphorical. Two more adjectives round out the picture. Parables are challenging and open-ended. First, the challenging part. They challenge the listener (or reader) to set scenes from his own life next to the parable and ask, "What would my life look like if I lived it in keeping with the kingdom of God?" The message most of us would like best is this: "Whatever you are doing in your life right now is God's will, because it is you who are doing it. So keep up the good work!" I ate lunch at a Chinese restaurant a few days ago. The noodles were rubbery, but the fortune in my cookie was fabulous. It confirmed what I have long suspected. "You are your own wisest counselor," it said! I'm not sure where fortune-cookie companies get their fortunes, but I don't think Confucius wrote that one. Jesus didn't write it, either, because confirming our complacency was the opposite of the purpose of his proverbial sayings and his parables. That's one reason, I suppose, they don't put the sayings of Jesus into fortune cookies that people eat before they pay the bill and add the tip.

The parables are not just vehicles for personal challenge. Recent scholarship highlights their role as social critics.[7] If they show what the kingdom of God is like, they also expose how sadly a dominant government or religion falls short of that kingdom. Recent scholars portray the parables as scenes of oppression of the poor and powerless by the rich and powerful in Jesus' day. Ruling political elites of the ancient world preserved their power by exacting tribute from the peasant class. Religious elites preserved their power by dictating who was an acceptable member of the religious community and who was not. There were two prominent categories of those who were excluded: the unclean and the sinners.

Drawing on ancient Israel's connection between cleanliness and holiness (Lev. 13:45–46; Deut. 23:10–11, 13–14), religious leaders designated certain people as unclean. Jesus discerned the truth that this category was not only a religious category but also a social category: one that often resulted from poverty, disease, and racial and gender prejudice. He addressed his ministry to those the religious elite classified as unclean: lepers (Mark 14:3), Gentiles (Mark 7:24–30), and women classified as "sinners" (Luke 7:36–50).

He also directed his ministry toward those the religious establishment classified as "sinners." Like "unclean," "sinner" in the ancient world was not just a moral category, but was also a social one. A widespread assumption in Jesus' day was that if you were poor or ill or physically impaired in some way, it was because you had sinned. If you were at the bottom of the social ladder, those who, in the Roman Empire were called "the expendables," it was because you deserved to be.[8]

Those who had no other options than to do the dirty, dangerous jobs no one else wanted to do were considered "sinners." This included tax collectors, shepherds, dung collectors, tanners, peddlers, weavers, bath attendants, and prostitutes. Jesus was speaking of this social category when he said, "I have come to call not the righteous but sinners" (Mark 2:17). He invited into his company those society labeled as unclean and as sinners. With his healings, his exorcisms, his table presence, and his teachings, both in short sayings and in longer parables, he proclaimed for them a kingdom, an empire of God. In God's empire, the means to life are free and accessible to all because they come from the gracious hand of God.[9]

Parables were about the kingdom of God, but not as a transcendent, abstract reality. They were about the kingdom of God as it breaks in upon, even while hampered by, oppression and injustice in everyday settings. Are we brave enough to open our minds to the parables' challenge to contemporary injustices? If so, we need to view them as social scenarios that exposed the contradictions between the actual situation of Jesus' hearers and God's desire for peace with justice. We need to turn their spotlight of social criticism on analogous contemporary scenarios.

Several of the parables that may have seemed harmless and bland to us before take on sharp and vivid contours when seen in this way. We wonder how Jesus' influential listeners would have reacted to a story of a feast to which the wealthy refuse to come, so the poor take their place. Or how about a story in which a rich man and a poor man die and their roles are reversed? What about a scene of a judge who didn't care about justice, but finally yielded to pestering? What about a scene in which the religious professionals fail to lend aid and a disreputable person stops without hesitation? What about a person who trades everything, all his earthly possessions, to buy a treasure that can never belong to him? We've said the parables are capable of an array of meanings. That array expands and sharpens when we allow a function of social critique to enter the mix.

Open-ended

So much for the "challenging" part of Jesus' parables. What about their open-ended quality? What about the fact that they give rise to just as many questions as answers? What about the fact that they can speak to a variety of situations in our personal, family, congregational, community, and national lives? Sometimes we would all like the luxury of meeting a complex reality with simplistic responses. Sometimes we all just want to say, "Never mind thinking for ourselves, just tell us what to do." "Help me out here. Exactly who is my neighbor?" "I am a busy person. Whom am I obligated to help, to love as I do myself, and whom can I cross off the list?" "OK, how many times do I have to forgive someone else before I can give up on them and move on to a more rewarding activity?"

I understand that the parables can be a frustrating teaching form for listeners who seek final, single meanings from every text because, sometimes, I am that listener. Once, after extended brow wrinkling and brain boggling, I actually thought I had grasped the essence of the parable of the Dishonest Steward. That euphoric feeling lasted about thirty seconds, and then was gone. Parable interpretation is like that. Just when we think we have pinned one down to a single definitive, permanent meaning, like a dead butterfly to a display board, it slips from our hands like the greased watermelon in the rugby game at the youth retreat. Since that is probably too many similes for one sentence, I'll tell a story instead.

I was once teaching a workshop on the parables at a laity education weekend. There were about twenty of us, and we had been talking about various interpretations of parables for the morning session and were about to break for lunch. We were in the middle of a lively, rich discussion of varying responses of class members to the parable of the workers in the vineyard. None of us in the group was quite prepared for the elderly gentleman sitting near the door to blurt out his negative feelings right before lunch. But that didn't stop him. "I have to say that I feel sorry for the original disciples if the parables were as complicated as we are making them!" he said. "The parables are simple stories with a single point. Why we are trying to make them so confusing is beyond me!" With that, he picked up his backpack and left in a huff, not returning after lunch. It was his loss.

Questions for Discussion

1. Why do you think Jesus chose parables to convey his vision of the kingdom of God?
2. Which one or two properties we discussed in this session seem most important to you in serving his purposes?

3

The Proclaimers of Jesus' Parables: Mark, Matthew, and Luke

Mark's Gospel

The Reign: The Kingdom of God in Mark

Mark's Gospel is a high-blood-pressure Gospel. The time is short and the stakes are high. Mark's Gospel, most scholars agree, was the earliest written of the four. It was probably written around 70 CE, shortly after the Temple in Jerusalem had been destroyed by the Romans. It reflects a time of imminent persecution for those who professed the Christian faith. They faced destruction and, in light of it, feared their efforts would prove paltry and futile. There is a consensus that Mark wrote at about the time of the First Jewish War (66–70 CE), toward the end of the reign of the Emperor Nero (54–68 CE) when Christians in Rome suffered terrible persecutions.[1] Speculation about the in-breaking of the kingdom soared at this time, as we can see from Mark 13, which is full of allusions to war and the destruction of the Temple in Jerusalem (Mark 13:14). Mark's Gospel (13:23) shares with Matthew's (24:36–44) an emphasis on the need for alertness, since the kingdom, ushered in by the Son of Man, will come at a time we do not expect.[2]

In Mark 12:28–34, a scribe comes to Jesus and asks him "Which commandment is the first of all?" Jesus answers with the Shema, the traditional Hebrew commandment to love God with one's whole being (Deut. 6:4–5). To that he adds, "You shall love your neighbor as yourself" (Lev. 19:18b), commenting that "There is no other commandment greater than these"

(Mark 12:31b). When the scribe earnestly agrees with him, Jesus commends him with these words: "You are not far from the kingdom of God" (Mark 12:34).

Jesus' series of parables about the kingdom of God in Mark 4 teach us that God's rule is "something hidden, indirect, surprising in its manifestation and not easily perceived."[3] The images are familiar. That tells us that the kingdom is near, breaking into the ordinary world where we dwell. The images also have a strangeness or improbability in them, conveying that the kingdom transcends our attempts to define it. The harvest is too great given the adversity that faces it. The mustard bush is a strangely diminutive metaphor for the grand traditional picture of God's reign. What we see is failure, hiddenness, and insignificance. God's purposes, though hidden, are still present, and we need to move toward them with confidence.

The Ruler: The Depiction of God in Mark

For members of Mark's community who feel out of control, Mark offers a depiction of God who, while mysterious, is solidly in control. There is a strong belief in the sovereignty of God in Mark—that nothing happens for good or for ill outside God's control. Jesus' often repeated predictions of his crucifixion and resurrection as events that "must happen" to fulfill God's purposes underscore that all is unfolding according to God's plans (Mark 8:31–32; 9:30–32; 10:32–34). The "secret," or mystery, of the kingdom of God that Jesus has given the disciples (though in Mark they never seem fully to grasp it) is the crucifixion and resurrection of Jesus (Mark 4:11). Mark encourages us to trust God and try to discern God's presence and work in small, surprising places, rather than in the obvious pomp and puffed-up power favored by the empires of this world.

Jesus' teachings and actions in Mark serve to point people, not to praise and worship him, but to obey God and to live in keeping with God's will as modeled by Jesus. Jesus' exorcisms and miracles draw attention to God, not to himself. They are thoroughly theocentric. The multiple references to "having faith" are to having faith, not in Jesus, but in God. Faith is faith in God and faith in the power of God at work through Jesus.[4]

And that faith will not always be easy. Christ is Israel's true king, but his kingship is hidden in suffering and rejection. In his suffering, the true nature of his kingship is revealed. Hence on the cross Jesus cries out, "My God, my God why have you forsaken me?" and a centurion declares, "Truly this man was God's Son!" (Mark 15:34, 39). Throughout Mark's Gospel, Jesus' kingship is shrouded and hidden, until he dies on the cross under the mocking banner "King of the Jews."[5] In Mark, Jesus tells people frequently to refrain from spreading the word of his messiahship (Mark 1:25; 5:43; 7:36; 8:30; 9:9). Jesus was probably reluctant to adopt the title because of its political, nationalistic connotations.[6] Because Mark, compared to the other evangelists, plays up this theme, scholars refer to it as Mark's "Messianic Secret" motif. It may be that Mark is trying to explain to his community why the whole world does not recognize Jesus' identity. What matters is that they do and that they persist in the face of opposition.

The Response: Discipleship in Mark

Usually, when a Gospel writer repeats themes or phrases, it is to give the reader the message that "This is important!" New Testament scholar Norman Perrin argues that Mark presents a pattern of preaching and being "delivered up." Mark tells us that John the Baptist preaches and (1:14) is "delivered up." Jesus preaches and (9:13) is "delivered up." Finally, Christians preach and can expect to be "delivered up" (13:9–13).[7]

Mark's spotlight on suffering may be due to the fact that in his community there were those teaching that, since Christ has been raised, we can expect triumph and rewards in this world. This perspective is called "triumphalism," and still shows up today in "prosperity preaching" that encourages us to "name it and claim it." In response Mark reminds his community that, like their Lord, they can expect persecution and should even be prepared for death.[8]

Mark wants us to look to Jesus to discern how to respond to both the presence and the promise of the kingdom of God. Jesus is the one who has the faith to discern God's kingdom in people and places the world viewed as beneath its notice, in the sacrifice of recognition and status for servanthood, and even in the sacrifice of his life as an expression of his love of God with his whole being and of his neighbor as himself.

How often have we longed to hear Jesus say to us, "You are not far from the kingdom of God!"? To get close to the kingdom we have to let go of a lot of baggage that normally fills the space in between us and the kingdom. That baggage includes, for one thing, our refusal to trust that God can bring redemptive outcomes from loss, failure, and death. That baggage also includes our habit of trusting appearances—so that whatever is large, whatever is rich, and whatever is powerful, fits our definition of success. Yet another piece of baggage is our habit of preoccupation with material possessions.

We are used to hearing commercials for drugs in which an actor, in a loud and confident voice, states for us all the drug's benefits. Only after the commercial, at a lower volume and much faster rate of speech, does the speaker list the drug's side effects. Trusting appearances and being preoccupied with material possessions have a very unattractive side effect: bloating of the ego. At the societal level, such values result in the emaciation of certain groups in society while others use a disproportionate amount of available resources.

In Mark 8:31–10:34, Jesus predicts his death and resurrection three times. After each prediction, one or more of the disciples objects (8:32b; 9:33–34; 10:35–37), because they don't think things need to spin out of control and go to such extremes. In each case, Jesus offers a correction. In all three cases, the disciples lack faith to trust God to work redemptive outcomes out of events that appear to be nothing but negative. In all three cases, Jesus' corrective teachings are similar to a lesson found in the miraculous harvest (Sower) and the mustard seed: "Don't trust appearances." He informs them that what looks like loss is actually gain in God's kingdom (Mark 8:33–38), that the greatest must be servant of all (10:38–40), and that they are called, not to lord it over others, but to welcome the little child in his name, which is a way of honoring both Jesus and the God who sent him (9:35–37).

Mark wants us to identify with Jesus' steady, sacrificial discipleship and to be warned by the disciples' repeated failures of discipleship. A feature of Mark's Gospel is that the disciples don't seem to advance much in their faith and understanding. By contrast, in Matthew, with its heavy emphasis on Jesus' teaching role, the disciples do make some progress (Matt. 20:24). In Mark, though, the disciples' unfortunate responses to Jesus' three predictions of his death and resurrection are meant to be cautionary tales for readers of the Gospel. And they aren't the disciples' only gaffes. They also display lack of faith in the two miracle-at-sea stories (4:35–41; 6:45–52), and, worst of all, they desert Jesus after dramatically promising that they will risk death rather than deny him in 14:26–31.

Fortunately, in Mark's Gospel, God is more gracious in forgiving thick-headed disciples than we ever are in forgiving one another. So the risen Jesus, in going before the disciples to Galilee (Mark 16:5–8), offers the gift of a divine purpose that is greater than our failures. Though the disciples in Mark struggled to believe his predictions and abandoned him in his time of pain, still he offers them a future pervaded by his presence and granted meaning by his mission.

Matthew's Gospel

The Reign: The Kingdom of God in Matthew

What Mark and Luke refer to as the "kingdom of God," Matthew calls the "kingdom of heaven," literally "kingdom of the heavens." This reflects the pious Jew's belief that it was irreverent to pronounce God's name directly.[9] The phrase refers to the ideal, future state when God's "will be done, on earth as it is in heaven." It occurs often in the Gospel of Matthew. It shows up five times in the Sermon on the Mount (5:10, 19, 20; 6:33; 7:21). It is the core of the message of John the Baptist (3:2), Jesus (4:17), and his disciples (10:7).

The kingdom of heaven belongs to those who are "poor in spirit," that is, those who realize their complete dependence on God for spiritual and physical sustenance (Matt. 5:3). Their needs for food, clothing, and sustenance will be met as they live single-mindedly and wholeheartedly for God's kingdom (5:3; 6:33). The kingdom also belongs to those who are "persecuted for righteousness' sake" (Matt. 5:10). Participation in the kingdom of heaven requires repentance (3:2; 4:17), hearing, doing, and teaching the commandments of God as expressed by Jesus (7:26). Entry into the kingdom of heaven requires living by God's commandments to love God with one's whole being and one's neighbor as oneself. This is the inward righteousness that exceeds the concern for ritual purity and religious observances of the Pharisees (5:19–20).

For Matthew, the kingdom of heaven is a reality that God has begun and sustains, that is already present in Jesus' teaching, healing, and exorcisms. It is also still to come. Jesus' ministry, including the parables, is our summons to respond by lives of profound and active righteousness, conduct focused on acts of mercy and hospitality toward others (7:21; 21:31b–32a).[10] When we live in such a way, we enter into the kingdom of heaven, as it is present now and as it takes shape in the future.

Gentiles as well as Jews can enter into this kingdom. Women as well as men are welcome in this kingdom. Matthew's genealogy of Jesus, with which his Gospel begins, includes four women, two of them Gentiles (Tamar, Rahab, the wife of Uriah [Bathsheba], and Ruth). His point is that God's plan of salvation includes Gentiles and that women can be positive examples of the surprising ways God works in history. Elsewhere in his Gospel, Matthew includes portraits of women who demonstrate bold initiative. Two examples are the Canaanite woman (15:21f.) and the woman who touches the fringe of Jesus' cloak (9:22). Matthew's message is that God uses those on society's sidelines to advance the plan of salvation.[11]

This fits Matthew's vision of the kingdom of heaven. He is convinced that, when it arrives, it will result in an order of life in which current roles and values are reversed. Possessions, prestige, and position will be turned on their heads. We can begin that reversal in our own lives now, on a voluntary basis, by becoming poor in spirit, by living in constant awareness of our need for God, and by acting on behalf of the poor and suffering. Or we can ignore this coming reality, content to give it lip service now and suffer the consequences later.

The Ruler: The Depiction of God in Matthew

The Gospel of Matthew begins and ends with the assurance that God is with us. Jesus' name Emmanuel means, "God is with us" (Matt. 1:23). The Gospel ends with the risen Jesus' words to the disciples: "And remember, I am with you always, to the end of the age" (Matt.

28:20). As in Luke and Mark, God sustains Jesus in the wilderness temptation (Matt. 4:1–11; Mark 1:12–13; Luke 4:1–13); God reveals Jesus' identity in the transfiguration (Matt. 17:1–8; Mark 9:2–8; Luke 9:28–36); and God is accessible to Jesus in prayer, through which he reveals knowledge of the Father to humankind (Matt. 11:25–30; Luke 10:21–22). As Jesus sends the twelve out to heal and exorcize, he assures them that God's Spirit will be with them (Matt. 10:20). For Matthew, Jesus' teaching function is a crucial avenue through which God's presence is revealed to us. God authorizes Jesus, his Son and Israel's Messiah, to teach with heavenly authority concerning the will of God (Matt. 5–7) and to perform miracles (Matt. 8–9). His miracles serve to give authority to his teachings.

God cares intensely for his children (Matt.10:29–30). Since God is sovereign, we live in utter dependence on God for material and spiritual sustenance. These twin realities are expressed by the Lord's Prayer in Matthew. The first three petitions affirm God's sovereignty: "Hallowed be your name," "Your kingdom come," and "Your will be done." The second three petitions express our dependence on God: "Give us this day our daily bread," "Forgive us our debts," and "Do not bring us to the time of trial."[12]

For Matthew, God, while a gracious initiator of relationship with us, is also a judge. In parables unique to Matthew's Gospel, the Last Judgment (Matt. 25:31–46) and the Unmerciful Servant (Matt. 18:23–34), as well as in Matthew's version of the Great Feast (Matt. 22:1–14), we experience the consequences of being hearers and not doers of God's will. Our shoulders may begin to slump beneath the weight of the Gospel's stress on God as inexorable judge. The parables of the Planted Weeds (Matt. 13:24–30) and the Vineyard Laborers (Matt. 20:1–15), unique to Matthew, seem to emphasize the forbearance and the graciousness of God. But even these end in visions of the judgment that comes to those who fail to respond to that patience and graciousness.

On the other hand, Matthew's Gospel does have Jesus as the Wisdom of God speaking of the yoke of obedience to him as easy and the burden as light (Matt. 11:28–30). It is also worth remembering that, in Matthew, obedience happens within a relationship that God both starts and sustains. For Matthew, "God with us" is both the beginning and the future of our story.

The Response: Discipleship in Matthew

Jesus' identity in Matthew is as Son of God and as Messiah. Matthew also depicts Jesus as a new Moses, a teacher of the law with unprecedented authority. It is no accident that he arranges Jesus' teaching material into five segments (Matt. 5–7; 13; 18; 19; 24–25). This is meant to remind readers of the five books of the Torah (Genesis, Exodus, Leviticus, Numbers, and Deuteronomy). What in Luke is the Sermon on the Plain in Matthew becomes the "Sermon on the Mount," pointing to mountains as traditional places of revelation and, in particular, to Mount Sinai, where Moses received the Ten Commandments.

In addition to depicting Jesus as a teacher with authority in interpreting the laws and commandments of Israel's Scripture and tradition (Matt. 7:29), Matthew plays up the role of Jesus as a teacher of wisdom, the art of moral discernment in daily life. He depicts Jesus as the Wisdom of God, as described in Proverbs 8:22–36 (see Matt. 11:19; 11:28–30; 23:34).[13]

Matthew's focus on a "higher righteousness" was apparently needed by his community, a mixture of Gentile and Jewish people, both of whom needed moral guidance. The Jewish group tended to feel they didn't have to do much, because their ritual observances and their identity as descendants of Abraham were their spiritual calling cards with God. The Gentile group rationalized that they didn't have to do much either, since the rituals and regulations of the Jewish members were not necessary for their membership in the community.

Matthew's Gospel was probably written by a Jewish Christian living about 85–90 CE. Some scholars theorize that Matthew's Christian-Jewish community was locked in conflict with a neighboring synagogue. Jesus' diatribes against the "scribes and Pharisees" in Matthew 23, then, would reflect the tension between Matthew and the rabbis of his own time rather than reporting verbatim interchanges between Jesus and Jewish leaders some fifty-five to sixty years earlier.[14]

Matthew invites both groups within his congregation, Jew and Gentile alike, to a "righteousness [that] exceeds that of the scribes and Pharisees" (Matt. 5:20). Righteousness is not mechanical obedience to rules or creative rationalization of what we are already doing. It is an inward faithfulness and obedience to the spirit of the law of God: love of God and love of neighbor (22:37–40). "Higher" righteousness does not mean that it is reserved for superior spiritual elite. "Higher" is better rendered "genuine," or "active." It links purity within to a passion for justice toward others. The Sermon on the Mount includes the warning, "Not everyone who says to me, 'Lord, Lord,' will enter the kingdom of heaven, but only the one who does the will of my Father in heaven" (7:21).

The Pharisees were one of many groups within Judaism in the late first century, and Matthew's quarrel was with only some within that group. The Pharisees were a sect of Judaism that existed, alongside many others, in Palestinian Jewish society from about 200 BCE to 100 CE. They were probably educated bureaucrats who served the ruling class. They sought to preserve Israel's identity by strict adherence to purity and Sabbath laws.[15] They were influential in Jewish society and were looked on favorably by at least some of the population, but their social status was not stable like that of hereditary or traditional leaders (priests, village elders). They were constantly recruiting new members and competing for influence with other groups and leaders. This fits the Gospels' depiction of the Pharisees as competing with Jesus and his followers and others for influence among the people.[16]

Their goal was to "make a fence for the law"—in other words, to protect it from infringement by surrounding it with specific rules of interpretation and application to daily life. Their original purpose was admirable, to enhance inward faithfulness to the law in daily life. In practice they had a tendency to multiply rules to the point that keeping the law could become a burden rather than a celebratory response to God's goodness. For example, tailors were not allowed to go out carrying a needle late in the day before the Sabbath, in case they were caught with it still in their pocket when the Sabbath began. They could go for a walk on the Sabbath day—provided it was not farther than two thousand cubits, roughly two-thirds of a mile, a distance determined by reference to the space between the people of Israel and the Ark of the Covenant when they first entered Canaan.[17]

Matthew's conflict with local Pharisees caused him to take three of Jesus' parables (the Vineyard Laborers, the Two Sons, and the Wicked Tenants)[18] and turn them into historical allegories about the recalcitrance of Israel and its replacement by the church in God's favor. For Matthew the church is the true Israel, replacing the old Israel in the center of God's purpose. Luke's message of universal salvation and the apostle Paul's assertion in Romans 12 that Israel is still within God's saving plan are good antidotes to Matthew's view.

We need to be very careful in studying Matthew, that we do not adopt his negative views toward a faction of the Jewish religion of his day and his location and generalize them to apply to the adherents of Judaism today. It is an unfortunate fact that Matthew's Gospel has been used to fuel the fire of anti-Semitism throughout the centuries.

Matthew is loyal to the Torah and to the spirit of Judaism's worship and devotional practices (Matt. 5:17–20). He is, at the same time, critical of its tendency, in some circles in his day, to focus on who is excluded rather than who is included and to be willing to settle for outward observances rather than inward devotion. For Matthew as for Mark, discipleship involves a purity of heart and not just of hands washed clean before eating (Mark 7:14–23; Matt. 15:10–20). Jesus emphasizes that the heart is the wellspring of good and evil actions alike. He criticizes acts of piety done with public pomp motivated by a desire for others' approval, rather than by devotion to God and neighbor (Matt. 6:1–18).

The harshness of Matthew's depiction of judgment is sometimes troubling. Elsewhere in the Gospels the phrase "weeping and gnashing of teeth," occurs only once, in Luke 13:28. But in Matthew it appears in the outcomes of several parables: the Weeds (13:42), the Fishnet (13:50), the Wedding Garment (22:13), the Faithful and Unfaithful Slaves (24:51), and the Talents (25:30). Matthew is not all in a minor key. In Matthew it is a gracious God who calls disciples and strengthens them, through prayer, to live obediently. In Matthew the Beatitudes, statements of blessedness, are not hoops we must jump through to win our salvation, but states of mind and spirit that are gifts to those who respond humbly to the nearness of God's presence and kingdom. Even in Luke's joyful, feast-filled Gospel, the Rich Man can't feast forever and ignore Lazarus without irreversible consequences.

Each evangelist told Jesus' story with the emphasis he felt his community needed to hear. If Matthew's congregation preferred performing perfunctory acts of piety to helping the poor, maybe they needed those repeated visions of gnashing of teeth and weeping. Maybe we do too. The task for today's readers of Matthew is to benefit from his accountability lessons, while affirming that it is a God of forgiveness and grace who holds us accountable.

Luke's Gospel

The Reign: The Kingdom of God in Luke

The Gospel of Luke is the first volume of a two-volume narrative of the lives of the founder and the first apostles of the Christian "Way." Luke believes that, in the births of John the Baptist and Jesus, a new age has dawned in the fulfillment of God's promises to his people Israel, the culmination of all that has gone before. It is the age of the Spirit, that mediates salvation for all people in an unrestricted expression of God's grace. Luke's first volume (The Gospel According to Luke) begins and ends in the temple of Jerusalem, while his second volume (The Acts of the Apostles) begins in Jerusalem and ends in Rome, the capital of the worldly empire. God's grace is good news for all who recognize their need for God's help, whatever their social status, gender, or nationality.[19]

Luke's Gospel features several themes with regard to the kingdom of God.

It will include non-Jews. This shows up in the positive portrayal Luke gives of Samaritans (Luke 10:29–37; 17:16; Acts 8:25).

It seeks to include outcasts and those on the margins of society (Luke 14:13, 21; 15:1–2; 17:11–12; 18:1–14; Acts 3:1–10).

We enter into the kingdom of God through persistent prayer (Luke 10:2; 11:13; 18:1–14; Acts 1:14; 2:42).

We enter into the kingdom of God through cautious, faithful use of our material possessions. A recurring theme for Luke is the danger of wealth and the proper use of possessions (Luke

12:13–21, 33–34; 16:1–13, 19–31; 19:1–10; Acts 2:43–45; 4:32–33; 5:1–10).[20]

The kingdom of God in Luke includes women as well as men. Luke's Gospel seeks to defend, reassure, and praise women. The "sinner" who anoints Jesus is contrasted with the Pharisee (Luke 7:36–50). The bent woman is given the unusual designation "daughter of Abraham" (Luke 13:16), affirming her dignity. The "impure" woman with the flow of blood is commended for her faith (Luke 8:43–48). The act of a woman listening to the teachings of Jesus is affirmed (Luke 10:38–42). Mary the mother of Jesus is viewed by Luke as significant, not just for her biological role, but because she is a model of obedient discipleship (Luke 1:38; 2:19, 51). The women who travel with Jesus and the Twelve and serve them are models of generosity (Luke 8:3). They are faithful witnesses to the crucifixion (Luke 23:49), the burial (Luke 23:55), and the angels at the empty tomb (Luke 24:23). In contrast to Mark's account (Mark 16:8), they do report what they have seen and heard "to the eleven and to all the rest" (Luke 24:9).[21]

The Ruler: The Depiction of God in Luke

Unique to Luke's Gospel are several parables that convey the character of God as merciful, compassionate, and forgiving. Rather than allegory, Luke's parables rely on realistic detail with regard to daily human life, and they offer paradigms of discipleship for daily Christian existence.[22]

God offers divine mercy to everyone. In Luke those who repent and turn around include a rebellious son, a wealthy tax collector, and a crucified criminal. In Acts, the centurion Cornelius and his household are converted, as is Saul. To both, God extends the offer to repent and be forgiven.[23]

Luke's parables often feature people behaving badly, perhaps to emphasize that God's mercy is for sinners. His parables feature a resentful older brother, a profligate younger brother, a ruthless boss, a dishonest manager, a corrupt judge, a greedy "rich man," a pompous Pharisee, and a dubious publican. We know that Luke's Gospel was written to a Gentile audience. These examples of repentance might have been especially needed by readers unfamiliar with the biblical tradition of repentance and turning back to God that would have been well known to Jews.[24]

God, as a gift of divine grace, through Jesus' ministry, gives forgiveness of sins to the repentant, casts out demons, and offers the gift of salvation through the bestowal of the Holy Spirit (Luke 11:13, 20; 19:1–9). The Holy Spirit comes upon John, Mary, Elizabeth, Zechariah, and Simeon in the first two chapters of Luke. It empowers and directs Jesus' ministry (Luke 3:16, 22; 4:1, 14, 18; 10:21). Jesus promises that God will give the Holy Spirit to those who prayerfully and persistenly seek God's aid (Luke 11:13). In Acts the Holy Spirit, identified as the Spirit of Jesus, inspires the apostles in their mission.[25]

God takes great joy in one lost sinner who repents. Chapter 15 of Luke, which includes several parables about losing and finding, underscores this facet of God's character.[26]

The Response: Discipleship in Luke

Discipleship for Luke is a matter of repentance and conversion, perseverance in faith, prayer, compassion, prudence in money matters, and joy.

Discipleship requires repentance and conversion. The words for "repentance" and "to repent" occur fourteen times in the Gospel of Luke and eleven times in Acts, almost half of the occurrences in the New Testament as a whole.[27] Lukan stories and parables that highlight repentance include the woman with the ointment (Luke 7:36–50), the parable of the Lost Son (Luke 15:11–32), the story of Zacchaeus (Luke 19:1–10), and the account of the penitent thief (Luke 23:39–43).

Luke's major parables feature a turning point, a crisis midway in the story. An internal dialogue of a main character often conveys the conversion experience. Examples include the Prodigal Son (Luke 15:11–32), the Dishonest Steward (Luke 16:1–8a), the Rich Farmer (Luke 12:16–20), and the rich man in the parable of the Rich Man and Lazarus (Luke 16:19–26).

For Luke, repentance is the only appropriate response to the dawn of the new age with the coming of the Messiah. It is a prerequisite of forgiveness and salvation, involving a change of heart and a change of life. Repentance and conversion anticipate the joy of the inbreaking of God's kingdom, which Luke often envisions as the festive sharing of food.[28]

To be a disciple means to exercise one's faith by perseverance. Luke emphasizes faith as perseverance because he is writing to a Greek and Roman context, in which there is opposition to confessing faith in Jesus and there are many other faiths to choose from. Faith must be able to withstand times of testing and temptation in full loyalty to God and his Christ. The uniquely Lukan parables of the Unjust Judge and the Friend at Midnight portray the perseverance that is necessary for discipleship in his context.[29]

The life of discipleship is a life of prayer. More than any other evangelist, Luke portrays Jesus at prayer. Jesus is habitually in deep communion with the Father, especially in moments of decision or testing in his life. He gives his disciples an example to follow. Like Jesus, the disciple is to live in the presence of God and to manifest this presence to others.[30] The way to eternal life leads through imitation of Jesus, the one who lived in the presence of God and came to seek and to save the lost (Luke 19:10). Following Jesus on the way involves both compassion for the suffering neighbor, as we see in the Good Samaritan parable (Luke 10:30–35), and attention to the teachings of the Lord, as we experience it in the uniquely Lukan story of Mary and Martha that comes right after it (Luke 10:38–42).

Luke's notion of discipleship carries a special concern for the poor and the socially outcast. This theme pervades his parables. Lazarus, the poor man, ends up in Abraham's bosom. Substitute guests feast at a grand banquet. A poor widow is vindicated by an unjust judge.[31]

We have mentioned that one of Luke's themes is the use of money and a right attitude toward material possessions. Several of Luke's parables involve trouble with money. The prodigal wastes it; a servant fails to invest it; a widow needs it; and a rich man will not share it with a beggar.[32]

In Luke, the disciple's response to God's kingdom involves joy. He holds out this joy because he writes to those who need to hear that it can help them transcend temptations and trials. A quarter of the references to joy in the New Testament occur in Luke-Acts. Joy has the first and last word in this Gospel, from the angels who announce "good news of great joy for all the people" (Luke 2:10), to the disciples who return to Jerusalem "with great joy" (Luke 24:52). Several of Luke's parables end on a note of joy. These include the parable of the Lost Sheep (Luke 15:4–7; Matt. 18:12–13), the Lost Coin (Luke 15:8–9), and the Lost Son (Luke 15:22–24, 32). The Great Feast parable in Luke ends with the poor dining on delicacies (Luke 14:16–24). Joy is a fundamental aspect of the Christian "Way," according to Luke. Repentance, conversion, prayerful perseverance in faith amid trials and temptations, compassion for the poor, prudence in money matters—all these lead to joy!

Questions for Discussion

1. How do you think the situation of the community to whom each evangelist was writing influenced his vision of the kingdom of God?
2. What themes characteristic of each Gospel do you think we especially need to hear today?

4

The Reign of God Is Not under Your Control

Parables from Mark

*B*eing in control is a crucial value in our society. A margarine with cholesterol-lowering benefits is called "Take Control." A large part of our fear of aging is the fear of being out of control—of our bodies, of our resources, and of where and how we will live. We want to control our money, our time, our relationships, our children, our parents, other drivers, our future. We even want to control God.

It was threatening to Jesus' first-century listeners to be told, through parables, that the kingdom of God was not and would not ever be under their control. It is no less threatening to us today. The news that the kingdom is not under our control contains both bad news and good news. The bad news is that the kingdom of God will most certainly threaten our security, to the extent that we have defined security as controlling our future, others' responses, and the results of our actions. The good news is that when we relinquish preoccupation with control in order to participate in the kingdom of God, our participation yields a harvest that is all out of proportion to the scope of our efforts.

Scholars identify six key Markan parables. They are the parable of the Sower (4:3–8), the Seed Growing Secretly (4:26–29), the Mustard Seed (4:30–32), the Wicked Tenants (12:1–11), the Fig Tree (13:28–29), and the Returning Master (13:34–36).[1]

In this session, we shall focus on the Sower, the Mustard Seed, and the Wicked Tenants.

The Sower
Mark 4:3–8 (Matt. 13:3b-8; Luke 8:5–8a)

Seeds are a good image to choose for a mysterious reality whose growth occurs without our instigation and, often, even without our knowledge.

Labels are very important in contemporary life. A label tells us what to expect inside a package. We can tell a lot about what we think a parable means by the label we put on it. Maybe "the parable of the Sower" is not the best, or at least the only, name for this parable. The sower is mentioned only briefly, when he scatters the seed in a careless, haphazard manner. He does not return to harvest it or to rejoice in the harvest.

The parable describes three failed sowings: The seed on the path is devoured by birds (Mark 4:4); the seed sown on rocky ground is scorched by the sun because it has no roots (vv. 5–6), and the seed sown among thorns is choked (v. 7). Some of the seed falls on good soil (v. 8).

One-fourth of the seed yields a harvest that is not just plentiful, but extraordinary. A tenfold yield was a good harvest, while a yield of seven and a half was an average one. The thirty-, sixty-, and one hundredfold harvests the parable describes are, literally, too good to be true.

There is a vast discrepancy between the three failures and the great harvest. The message to Jesus' disciples is that what God has begun in his ministry, despite repeated apparent failures, will have ultimate success. By his view, we might call the parable "the parable of the Successful Harvest."

Biblical scholar J. Dominic Crossan emphasizes that it is not so much the size of the harvest that counts, but the fact that it happens at all. However big or small the harvest, against such opposition there is a miraculous quality to it: it is a gift whose graciousness and surprise are meant to make us think of the kingdom of God.[2] By his view, we ought to call this parable "the parable of the Miraculous Harvest."

The parable of the Seed Growing Secretly (Mark 4:26–29) follows the parable of the Sower. It emphasizes that it is not our knowledge or actions that ultimately bring about the growth of the seeds, but it is our responsibility to harvest the crop. This brief parable has an air of great urgency, which fits the probable context in which Mark was written.

Allegory of the Seeds
Mark 4:14–20

The parable of the Sower is followed by a passage (vv. 10–20) in which Mark depicts Jesus as turning from addressing large crowds to speak to a more intimate group. He offers an allegorical interpretation of Mark 4:3–8. An allegory, as we have already noted, is a story in which each figure and feature actually refers to something else beyond the story. Allegories can be used as codes for oppressed groups to communicate with one another during times of persecution.

The word choices and themes of the allegorical explanation of the Sower reveal that it is probably the product of the early church. Jesus' parable in vv. 3–8 is about how his listeners are to respond to God. The church's appended explanation of his parable in vv. 13–20 reflects how various groups responded to Jesus' teachings about the kingdom of God. It also reflects the challenges to faith posed by persecution and possessions that were operative in Mark's community.

Verses 10–12 are confusing. They sound like a clear statement that Jesus uses parables intentionally so that he can reach some and not others. The quotation in verse 12 is from Isaiah 6:9–10, the call story of Isaiah. Just after he accepts God's call, Isaiah is told that his ministry will not be well received. In fact, it seems as if his calling is to preach to a faithless people. My interpretation is that "in order that" in verse 12 is better rendered "with the result that." A typical construction in Hebrew is to use a command to express a result. Jesus is not saying he uses parables deliberately so some will be excluded. He is acknowledging that some will see and hear, but will not, at a deeper level, understand and take his words to heart.[3]

Verses 10–12 then, rather than being a statement of divine intention that some not hear, is a description of the mixed reception of any prophet's life and teachings, whether those of Isaiah, whose words these verses cite, or of Jesus. The "secret of the kingdom of God" referred to in verse 11 is the cross and resurrection of Jesus Christ, a real-life parable of the victory of God's kingdom over circumstances in which death and failure seem to have had the last word.

The seed parables point us to hidden realities whose power and activity will one day be manifested. They remind hearers and readers of Jesus' ministry: its power was hidden on the cross, glimpsed in the resurrection, and is now growing steadily in the world. This is all despite the appearance of initial failure and current domination, whether by the Roman Empire of Mark's day or the variety of forms of empire in our day.

Mark uses the seed parables to define discipleship as hearing, accepting, and bearing fruit, following the way of Jesus, which yields a bountiful harvest. In all of this, we are not to forget that it is God's power, not our own efforts at control, that gives the growth. Says biblical scholar John Donahue, "The miracle and mystery of growth provide a polyvalent cluster of images which evokes God's power and graciousness in all areas of life."[4]

The Mustard Seed
Mark 4:30–32 (Matt. 13:31–32; Luke 13:18–19)

The parable of the Mustard Seed (Mark 4:30–32) contrasts the smallness of the mustard seed, characterized as the smallest of all seeds, with the size of the final tree. We have said that parables paint scenes from the natural world, but always with a strange twist or incongruous detail. They are, to quote C. H. Dodd's definition, "realistic, yet strange." The detail that doesn't fit in this parable is the fact that the mustard seed doesn't really grow into a tree large enough for birds of the air to nest in its branches. That detail would better fit a large tree. This extravagant detail is meant to remind us of the kingdom of God, which, while it has small beginnings, has surprising results.

The phrase "the birds of the air can make nests in its shade [or branches]" is a clue that connects this parable with several Old Testament passages where trees are used as grand, dramatic metaphors. Israel is depicted as a noble cedar in Ezekiel 17:22–24. "In the shade of its branches will nest winged creatures of every kind" (v. 23b). Assyria (Ezek. 31:6) and Babylonia (Dan. 4:12) are both portrayed using the metaphor of a cedar tree, lofty and proud, in whose branches the birds of the air nested, but whose pride will lead to their downfall. The righteous person who trusts in God is compared to a flourishing tree in Psalms 1:3, 92:13–15, and Jeremiah 17:7–8.[5]

Parables, rather than being simple stories with one point, are complex scenarios that can evoke all kinds of connections, not only with daily life, but with other texts. So the humble mustard seed that becomes a shrub could make us think of God's care for us like a flourishing tree, or it could turn our minds to the fact that the mustard shrub is not going to be like the mighty trees or empires of former times, which grew through power and violence.

The images of the seed parables in Mark 4 are realistic and yet strange. Miraculous harvests don't happen in adverse conditions, and a scruffy shrub seems like an odd choice as a metaphor for God's kingdom when one could have chosen a magnificent cedar. Jesus' parables call his audience to expect the in-breaking of God's reign into our ordinary daily lives. They also call us to remember that the kingdom of God has its own time and rate of growth. They call us, in John R. Donahue's words, "to look beyond what we see to what we hope for."[6]

In Mark's Gospel several characters who are insignificant and not even disciples are praised for their faith, while the disciples often fall short. These commendable cameos include the paralytic's friends (Mark 2:1–5), the Gerasene demoniac (Mark 5:18–20), Bartimaeus (Mark 10:51–52), the scribe (Mark 12:32–34), the woman with the ointment (Mark 14:3–9), women disciples at the crucifixion (Mark 15:40–41), and Joseph of Arimathea (Mark 15:43–46).[7] These persons are living parables, mustard seeds that grow into examples of faith that can nurture future would-be disciples.

We twenty-first-century types want to be in control. We want our lives to be full of successes and significance. Jesus calls on us to have more patience with and respect for failure, hiddenness, and insignificance. For they point beyond themselves toward the reality of the kingdom of God already in our midst.

The Wicked Tenants
Mark 12:1–8 (Matt. 21:33–39; Luke 20:9–15a)

This has always been one of my least favorite parables. It seems like such an obvious allegory of the rejection of Jesus, eight verses that seem to hold little positive value and that have been used to inflict much harm through the anti-Semitic preaching they have fueled through the centuries.

As we have already mentioned, a version of this parable appears in the *Gospel of Thomas*. There it refers simply to a "son," rather than a "beloved son," which is a clear reference to Jesus. It omits the reference to the closing actions of the vineyard owner, destroying the tenants and giving the vineyard "to others." Instead the parable ends with the actions of the tenants in killing the owner's son and the implied question "What then will the vineyard owner do?" (Mark 12:9a).

We know what we would do—go and get revenge on these tenants for destroying the son. But in this earlier, shorter version of the parable, we no longer see it as it is presented in Mark, as an allegorical reprimand of Israel for rejecting Jesus. Its abrupt ending leaves it up to the listeners to decide what they think will be the consequences of the tenants' actions.

It is realistic that a vineyard owner would send a servant to tenants to collect his share of the produce of the vineyard. It is even realistic that the tenants would resent the vineyard owner, who had perhaps bought up their family plots and turned them into a vineyard, a common practice at the time. It would have made more profit for him and it would also have the advantage of increasing his power over those who worked the land. It made them dependent tenants rather than independent landowners of small family plots. It is strange that the tenants would repeatedly mistreat and even kill his emissaries without any reprisal by the vineyard owner.

The parable as we have it in Mark ends with the owner's destruction of the tenants and giving the vineyard to others. And, when we read it, we may think, "Yes, that's the way it should be. People who reject God and who mistreat others ought to face the consequences." In the earlier version, we aren't told what the vineyard owner will do, and we aren't told what the tenants will do next. We remember that the parables are Jesus' answers to the question "What is the kingdom of God like?" And we are focusing on one answer, as illustrated by some of the key parables in the Gospel of Mark: "It is not and never will be under your control." So perhaps this parable has something to say about the fact that we cannot control God's merciful, continual outreach to others. Even though we know full well that they have used up all nine of their lives and all three of their strikes, we are not the ones who get to say when they have used up all their chances with God. Even though they have pushed their luck, blown their opportunities, gotten on our last nerve, and brought us to the end of our rope, we can't call a halt to the height, depth, or duration of the mercy of God. And the same is true when we turn our eyes from others to the person in the mirror.

What implications might this parable hold for our personal and public lives? What would this parable have to say to that troubling relationship we have with our child, our parent? What does it have to say to our inability to forgive ourselves? What does it have to say to us as we live knowing that someone whose opinion matters deeply to us condemns us in some central way? What does this parable have to do with our reflection on the criminal justice system, the death penalty? What relevance might it have to our responsibility to help people in our society who, some would say, have brought their troubles on themselves? The wicked tenants try God's patience. So do we. We don't know how they will respond next to the extended, undeserved mercy of God. How will we?

Even without Mark's specific statement of the vineyard owner's actions, those listening, if they had applied the parable to their own actions with regard to Jesus, would have been angry. The parable has a bite to it no matter how you look at it.

The Returning Master (or The Doorkeeper) Mark 13:34–36 (Luke 12:35–38)

This parable is an allegory composed by Mark to convey a lesson to his community about life between the resurrection and the return of Jesus. It tells us that a man, who we later find out is the lord of the house, goes on a journey. This is a familiar metaphor for the absence of Jesus before his return. While he is gone he entrusts his authority (*exousia*) (Mark 13:34) to his servants. The *authority* or *power* of Jesus is an important concept for Mark. Jesus' first appearance in the Gospel is as one who teaches with authority (Mark 1:22, 27) and as one who has authority to forgive sin (Mark 2:10). Jesus, in calling his disciples, bestows power (*exousia*) on them (Mark 3:15; 6:7).

Those who wait are described as servants (*douloi*). Servanthood is also a crucial concept for Mark. Power or authority for Mark is to be expressed in servanthood. Jesus commands the disciples to be servants of all (Mark 9:35), in imitation of the Son of Man who came not to be served but to serve (Mark 10:45).[8] Discipleship entails a deliberate relinquishing of authority to Jesus so that we may serve him and, in serving him, serve others. We prepare for his return by giving up our preoccupation with controlling our lives, and embarking on lives dedicated to serving others. That way, whenever he comes, he will find us alert and at our posts.

Mark's use of the metaphor of the house reflects the house church to which Mark wrote and is a metaphor for the community, the church itself.

Questions for Discussion

1. Where do you experience the kingdom of God present in small, seemingly insignificant ways in your church and community?
2. In what ways should we relinquish control over outcomes in our lives so God's outcomes can come to fruition?

5

The Reign of God Shows Up where You Least Expect It

Parables from Luke

The Good Samaritan
Luke 10:30–35

The story with which our study began mentioned a man reading a detective novel while riding a train through the Alps. When asked how he could ignore the stunning vistas beyond the train compartment he replied, "I've taken this trip so often I have seen it all." Many people feel this way about the Good Samaritan, more than any other parable except perhaps the Prodigal Son. We think we already know all there is to know about it. This is how we think it goes: A lawyer comes to Jesus trying to trip him up with questions about eternal life and who is his neighbor. Jesus then tells a story that has a Samaritan as the hero, which would have shocked Jews who, at that time, hated Samaritans. The realistic part of the parable is that a person on a journey gets beaten up and, subsequently, other people walk by without helping. The strange part is who sees and walks by and who sees and stops to help. Jesus' listeners would expect the Jewish religious leaders to see, stop, and help. They would not expect this of a Samaritan.

We are quite familiar with the traditional boiling down of the parable's message to an example story: Don't be like this. Be like this. "Don't be self-righteous, assuming God can't work through people you look down on. And be like the Samaritan, helping those you meet each day who need your help."

There is some truth there. But the familiar interpretation doesn't do justice to the rich texture of the parable. So let's pose the question to the parable: "What is the kingdom of God like?" And let's try on my answer, "It shows up where you least expect it." And let's see if any new details in the landscape appear. The context of the parable is a question to Jesus from a student of Torah (a lawyer) in Luke 10:25–28. The lead-in to the parable tells us that the lawyer "stood up to test Jesus" (10:25). Some interpreters assume he doesn't really want to know the answer, but that he just wants to test the teacher or stand out in the crowd. They give him no benefit of the doubt. They lump him together with the self-righteous people to whom Jesus tells the story of the Pharisee and the tax collector in Luke 18:9. Or they group him with the spies who try to trap Jesus in the question about the lawfulness of paying taxes to Caesar in Luke 20:20–26.[1]

But what if the lawyer had mixed motives? What if, in addition to wanting to test Jesus, his questions are motivated by a desire to be directed by him? What if this Torah student actually wants to know the answer to the question "What must I do to inherit eternal life?" Or what if he wants to hear what he knows is the answer from the Torah confirmed on the lips of one whom many look up to as their teacher? Jesus asks his question back to him, assuming that, as a student of Torah, he should already know the answer. The lawyer answers with the command to love God and neighbor from Deuteronomy 6:5 and Leviticus 19:18. Jesus affirms his answer and tells him that if he does this he will live.

Then the lawyer asks a follow-up question, the text says because he wanted "to justify himself." If individuals want to "justify themselves," they want to be perceived as good and just, to be viewed as guiltless and righteous, to be approved and accepted. The lawyer wanted Jesus' acceptance and approval. He wanted to stand out from the crowd in Jesus' estimation. I have found over the years that students will go to great lengths to gain the teacher's approval. Any teacher will tell you, though, that the best way a student can impress a teacher is by doing the readings, knowing the material, and being able to talk about its practical impact on daily life. Students still sometimes resort to other means. They may bring the teacher food items that she has mentioned in passing are her favorites. I hasten to say that, while I enjoyed the apple fritters and the peanut M&Ms, I have never requested such items or so much as implied that placing them in my campus mailbox would improve a student's grade! Sometimes students ask if they can do extra-credit work if their last assignment received a poor grade. They may come to class early to help set up the chairs. If they come in late, while the class is discussing this week's readings, they may immediately jump in and try to contribute to the conversation, never mind that they haven't done the readings, because class participation is 10 percent of the final grade.

One other way students try to gain a teacher's approval is by asking what they regard as a nuanced, subtle question in class, which they hope will reveal their intellectual depth. I wonder why the lawyer felt a need to justify himself to Jesus. And I wonder what answer he was hoping for to his question "Who is my neighbor?" A list of categories of people he needed to try to love as he loved himself, the shorter the better? Is the lawyer a human being like the rest of us who wants to know the bare minimum the syllabus requires to pass the course?

If it is true that the kingdom of God shows up where we least expect it, and I believe that it is, then maybe we meet it first in the gap between our knowing what God requires of us with regard to our fellow human beings and our willingness to do it. Maybe our fear that we are falling short is an entry point for the kingdom of God in our lives. The lawyer, thanks to Jesus' interpretation of Torah, is confirmed in what he was afraid was true. That is, that entering into the kingdom of God, inheriting eternal life, means a wholehearted, singleminded devotion to God that overflows from our hearts, minds, souls, and strength in practical, loving deeds done on behalf of our fellow human beings. This is an assignment that no syllabus can contain, that is not done to impress a teacher but to express the love of God.

Parables scholar Luise Schottroff, in her interpretation of this parable, connects the lawyer's question with the question asked by various groups of people in Luke 3:10, 12, 14, responding to John the Baptist's preaching: "What should we do?" She believes that concrete, action-oriented question is the fundamental question answered by the study of Torah. That study "is not aimed at timeless ethical doctrine but at the concrete situation of those who ask, What is the action God expects, here and now?" She believes that this parable belongs within "the rich Jewish tradition of active compassion as an expression of love for God. Love for God and doing justice go together."[2]

Other parables that feature this same emphasis include the parable of the Rich Man and Lazarus, another parable unique to Luke (16:19–26) and the parable of the Judgment from the twenty-fifth chapter of Matthew.

There are several things the parable of the Good Samaritan doesn't tell us. It doesn't tell us that the man in the ditch was a Jew. It doesn't tell us why the priest and the Levite did not stop to help him. Some scholars have theorized that their ritual purity regulations prohibited them from contact with a corpse. Did they assume he was dead, or did they get close enough to see that he was still alive, and still decide not to help? We don't know. The parable doesn't tell us why the Samaritan was moved with pity. It does spend quite a bit of energy specifying the concrete actions he took to help the injured man.

The emphasis in this parable is not on helping us determine whom we are to view as our neighbor and to whom we are to show love. Its focus is on the kind of people we are to be, active neighbors, as we live on the lookout for those in need of help. The parable says, of all three observers of the man in the ditch, that they "saw him." The first two engaged in a twofold action. They "saw him" and then, in response to that sighting, they "passed by on the other side." The response of the third person was threefold. He "saw him," he was "moved with pity" and then he took concrete action to express his compassion and assist the injured man. This parable is not a general lesson in loving humanity or loving one's enemies. It is a specific scenario in which a teaching about active compassion, shared by the Hebrew Scriptures and the teachings of Jesus, becomes a deed.[3]

The sequence of seeing, having compassion, and acting is a common one in the Gospels. In Luke's Gospel, when Jesus "saw" the woman weeping at the death of her only son, he "had compassion for her" and brought her son to life (Luke 7:13). When the father "saw" the prodigal son "still far off, . . . [he] was filled with compassion" and ran and embraced him (Luke 15:20). Matthew and Mark repeatedly tell us that Jesus himself, when he "saw" the crowds, had compassion on them and healed, fed, and taught them (Matt. 9:36; 14:14; 15:32; Mark 6:34; 8:02). In the parable of the Last Judgment in Matthew 25:31–46, what makes some blessed is the fact that, though they didn't realize it, in seeing the poor and helping them they saw and helped Jesus. By contrast, what makes others cursed is that they never really did see Jesus suffering and in need because they never really saw the poor.

A final thing the parable doesn't tell us is whether the lawyer did as Jesus told him to, "Go and do likewise" (Luke 10:37). The outcome of the parable is now up to us, as contemporary people, characterized by the same combination of sincerity and shallowness as the first-century lawyer.

The Rich Man and Lazarus
Luke 16:19–26

Unlike other parables we have explored, this one does not stay in the realm of first-century village life. It spans this life and the next. It is realistic in its portrayal of the vast gap between rich and poor. The phenomenon of the poor waiting for crumbs at the doors of the rich is a detail taken straight from first-century life. It is strange in that the reversal of fortunes it depicts contradicts the widespread belief that wealth was a sign of God's favor and poverty a sign of sin. The story reflects the ancient belief that the righteous and the wicked can see each other after death.

The background of this parable is a tale from Egyptian folklore about the reversal of fates after death. It also has connections to rabbinic stories. In Greek the name *Lazaros* has the same root consonants as the name *Eliezer* who, Genesis 15:2 tells us, was a servant of Abraham. Some rabbinic tales feature Eliezer (Greek *Lazaros*) walking in disguise on the earth and reporting back to Abraham on how his children are observing the Torah's prescriptions regarding the treatment of the widow, the orphan, and the poor. Lazarus is a poor beggar (Luke 16:20); he returns to Abraham's bosom, and the rich man requests that Abraham send him as an emissary to his brothers (Luke 16:27–28).[4]

This parable is found only in Luke. It underscores a theme expressed earlier in the Gospel (Luke 1:52). God has "brought down the powerful from their thrones, and lifted up the lowly." The story is a three-act play. The first act portrays the earthly contrast between the wealthy man and Lazarus. The second act describes the reversal of their conditions in the afterlife. The third act depicts the rich man's request to Father Abraham for a sign so that those still living can avoid his torment, a request that Abraham refuses.

First-century hearers of this parable would not have assumed that the rich man was evil and that the poor man was righteous. On the contrary, as we noted, wealth in the ancient world was often viewed as a sign of divine favor, while poverty was viewed as evidence of sin. The rich man's sin was not that he was rich, but that, during his earthly life, he did not even "see" Lazarus, despite his daily presence at the entrance to his home. The first time he ever notices Lazarus is from Hades, when "he looked up and saw Abraham far away with Lazarus by his side" (16:23).[5]

As for Lazarus, we aren't told he was pious, but his name means "God helps," which implies righteousness. Lazarus' hunger and willingness to eat whatever was at hand (Luke 16:21) are reminiscent of the younger son's famished, desperate condition in Luke 15:16.[6]

The rich man calls Abraham his "father." Earlier in Luke (3:8) we get the message that claiming a religious heritage cannot by itself gain us salvation. Living a life characterized by active compassion toward others is a sign that we are responding to God's covenant. John the Baptist tells the crowds, "Bear fruits worthy of repentance. Do not begin to say to yourselves, 'We have Abraham as our ancestor'; for I tell you, God is able from these stones to raise up children to Abraham" (Luke 3:8).

What is it that causes some people to have something or someone in their line of vision and yet not really see them? And what causes others who have someone or something in their line of vision to really see them? What makes the difference between not really seeing and seeing? We have said that this parable is one of several in Luke that conveys the truth that the kingdom of God shows up when and where we least expect it. We don't expect it to show up in the gap between the bearable, even pleasant or luxurious, living conditions of some and the unbearable, inhumane living conditions of others. We don't expect it to show up in the opportunity to see that gap and to move from seeing to active compassion before it is too late. But we ought to have learned by now that the kingdom of God is not a prisoner to our expectations.

I mentioned earlier that the story of the Rich Man and Lazarus reflects the ancient belief that the righteous and the wicked can see each other after death. If they are attentive to the presence of the kingdom of God, they can also see each other before death!

The Pharisee and the Tax Collector Luke 18:10–14a

This parable is a parable of two men who each offer prayers, with surprisingly different results. It reveals a couple of Luke's favorite foci: on prayer and on God's mercy to outcast sinners. It reveals the combination of realistic, yet strange, details and the presence of paradox to undercut conventional understandings of the kingdom of God. That two people go to the temple to pray, one of them a Pharisee, is unremarkable. What is strange is that one of them is a tax collector. Tax collecting was one of the occupations forbidden to Jews. Tax collectors were viewed as ritually impure and as dishonest. In a country exploited through widespread taxation, they were highly unpopular.[7] The paradox in the parable lies in the fact that someone viewed so negatively by the established religion and people generally should be the one "justified," that is, accepted, by God for his prayer. The other half of the paradox is that someone viewed positively by the people, the Pharisee, should behave in a blatantly self-righteous manner.

Before the destruction of the Second Temple in Jerusalem in 70 CE, the Pharisaic way of life was practiced by a relatively modest group of men and women. It had no political power. It was favored by the people because it took Jewish tradition and the Torah seriously and tried to interpret and live them in ways that touched daily life. The Pharisees taught the people to regard the gathering around the household dinner table as a community of worship. The handling of food and dishes were religious activities.

After the destruction of the temple in 70 CE, when the institutions of Jewish life were disrupted by Roman violence, the Pharisaic tradition of teaching and living was a force that enabled the survival of the people.[8]

We must not make the mistake so many interpreters of this parable have made, assuming that the Pharisee in the parable is representative of all Pharisees, that it was a religious movement founded on works alone and despising others.The story is not intended to show, illustrated by this one Pharisee, that this is how all Pharisees are. This negative perspective on this parable and on Pharisees in general is reflected by our common use of the word *pharisaical,* which we take as synonymous with self-righteousness. The listeners of Jesus' day would have expected the Pharisee to be a careful observer of the Law, in keeping with their generally high view of the Pharisaic movement. They would not expect the tax collector to go to the temple at all. The parable serves up two behaviors that are out of character: that the Pharisee prays in a self-righteous manner, and that the tax collector prays at all!

The contrast between the two prayers is marked. The Pharisee stands apart, probably so that his litany of virtues can be heard by other worshipers and by the tax collector. The Pharisee's prayer keeps the focus on himself. It is "I" this and "I" that. His list of virtues divides the community rather than unifying it. It perpetuates the us/them dichotomy we often use in thinking of other people.

The tax collector stands on the margins, "beating his breast." This is a physical gesture associated with women rather than men in the ancient Near East, emphasizing the unexpected nature of his actions. He keeps his head bent. His words are simple. He does not embark on an eloquent litany of his sins to match the Pharisee's virtues. He hopes in God alone, not in an extravagant outpouring of remorse. Like other powerless outsiders in Luke and in the Old Testament—the poor, the widow, the stranger—the tax collector casts himself on the mercies of God, and God hears and upholds his prayer.

I am quick to identify with the tax collector, not for his being hated by his community, not for his unpleasant profession, but because God liked his prayer better. It would be different if I thought I was in any way favored by God over others, or even wished to be. It would be different if I were proud of my adherence to moral values, and felt this made me better than other people and more deserving of God's attention and salvation. If I had any of those kinds of thoughts, then I can see how I might identify with the Pharisee in the parable.

The lead-in to the parable speaks volumes: "He . . . told this parable to some who trusted in themselves that they were righteous and regarded others with contempt" (Luke 18:9). If we are prone to the dangers of pride and self-righteousness, the parable calls us to look over in the corner to where our teacher stands with bent head. For the tax collector becomes the teacher of the Pharisee in the parable. The invitation to enter into the kingdom of God shows up where we least expect it. It shows up within ourselves, in the ember of humility that still burns, yet that needs to be fanned to warm and illuminate our inner life. In our families, our churches, our communities, the gate to the kingdom of God opens before us in the example of those who are humble before God.

Questions for Discussion

1. Where do we see a gap between our compassion for others and what Jesus asks of us in our daily lives?
2. Who has been your teacher in the lesson of humility before God and others?
3. Why do some see and have compassion on the suffering of others, while others barely even notice? How have we responded in both ways in our lives?

6

The Reign of God Shows Up where You Least Expect It

Parables from Matthew

The Ten Bridesmaids (or The Closed Door) Matthew 25:1–12

One of the themes dear to Matthew's heart is the theme of the anticipation of coming judgment. It is important for him to emphasize to his community two things with regard to Jesus' return: One is that they don't know when it will come, so speculation is futile. The second is that it will come, so preparation is crucial. In the parable of the Faithful and Unfaithful Slaves that directly precedes the parable of the Closed Door, the master comes back sooner than the slave anticipated and found him abusing his powers. In this parable, the bridegroom comes later than the foolish bridesmaids anticipated and they had not gathered the provisions needed to welcome him.

Despite our constant preoccupation with the future, we are often unprepared for what comes next in life. Sometimes a premature ending takes us by surprise. At other times, we are unprepared for something to take longer than we had anticipated. In the former case, we may think we have all the time in the world—to mend a relationship, to achieve an important goal, to discontinue a bad habit or begin a good one, to take care of ourselves, to develop our relationship with God, to read important books, to take a stand, to show we care. My paternal grandmother lived to be ninety-five. My father looked very much like his mother, so naturally I just always assumed that he, too, would live to be ninety-five. Until he got liver cancer at age seventy-four and died at age seventy-six. I felt robbed of twenty years. Where is the time now to express my appreciation to him, to call him and ask his advice on this or that? We have all the time in the world to spend time with our kids. Except that somebody sped up the clock, and now their rooms are empty and we get the sinking feeling that a ship has sailed that will never return to port. There I go mixing metaphors again, but I have a lifetime to get over that bad habit and all my others as well.

I was once in a hotel workout room, its sole occupant, walking on the treadmill in between meetings and reading a light novel. A man came in and got on the elliptical machine. He tried watching CNN for a while, but soon got bored, and so became determined to engage the only other person in the room in conversation. "My wife makes me come down here every day. I hate this. What are you reading?" I showed him the cover. "You seem pretty fit, but you won't live forever," he said to me. "Shouldn't you be reading something more important?" I started to point out that he hadn't brought anything to read at all, but put aside the impulse. He was right. I may live quite a while, but I will die not having read all the important books. Maybe there is more urgency to try than I usually feel.

Rabbi Eliezer taught his disciples, "Repent one day before your death." One of them then asked, "How will we know when that day is?" To which he replied, "All the more reasons to repent today, lest you die tomorrow."[1]

In the parable of the Closed Door, the problem was not a surprisingly quick return of the master, but his surprising delay. The bridesmaids, the five foolish ones anyway, were not prepared for the long haul. Many of us don't have health habits made for the long haul. We have fad diets and sporadic exercise regimes. Many of us don't participate in friendships for the long haul, but allow geographic changes to end friendships we thought would be lifelong. Maybe we experience surges of outrage at the injustice in our world, but do we have the passion for justice to sustain a lifetime of advocacy and activism? Even though life and the world may seem to go on forever, a day is coming when there will be no more second chances to do certain things or to cease doing others.

This parable of the Ten Bridesmaids appears only in Matthew's Gospel. Certain features of the wedding it describes seem realistic, others are strange. In ancient Palestinian weddings the marriage feast was at night; the bridegroom was met with lamps, and the bridegroom did delay coming for the bride.[2] Certain details are not realistic: they include the length of the delay, the midnight arrival, and the supposition that the shops would have been open for the sleeping maidens to buy oil (see Luke 11:5–8).[3]

The parable is an allegory of the delay of Christ's return in Matthew's community. Those awaiting the return of the groom are called "virgins." Virginity is commended, because the assumption was that the unmarried person is concerned for the things of the Lord rather than the needs of a spouse (Matt. 19:10–12). The five virgins who are prepared for the return symbolize appropriate Christian discipleship during the delay of the return of Christ.[4]

The five foolish maidens are not foolish because they slept, but because their lamps are not lit. Light in the parable symbolizes good deeds done in response to God's gracious initiative. In Matthew 5:14–16, Jesus exhorts his disciples, "Let your light shine before others, so that they may see your good works and give glory to your Father in heaven." In 13:43, Matthew's Jesus says that "The righteous will shine like the sun in the kingdom of their Father." "Light" (see Mark 4:22; Luke 11:33) is a symbol of good deeds or proper moral disposition.[5]

The return of Christ, for Matthew, will be a time that separates the good from the bad (Matt. 13:36–43; 25:31–46). The five wise virgins and the five foolish virgins represent these two groups. In the conclusion to the Sermon on the Mount in Matthew, Jesus says, "Not everyone who says to me, 'Lord, Lord,' will enter the kingdom of heaven, but only the one who does the will of my Father in heaven. On that day many will say to me, 'Lord, Lord. . . .' Then I will declare to them, 'I never knew you; go away from me, you evildoers'" (Matt. 7:22–23). In this parable, the bridesmaids cry out, "Lord, Lord" and the bridegroom answers, "I do not know you" (Matt. 25:12).

I have said that one of the answers the parables give to the question "What is the kingdom of God like?" is this: "It shows up where you least expect it." In this case, it is the vision of a door slammed in our faces and permanently locked, a door that, for so long, was completely open to us. Every shattering of the illusion of endless time, every reminder of the ticking clock and our mortality, is where the kingdom of God beckons.

I once led a yearlong spirituality class with about a dozen students committed to the practices of Christian prayer. Over the Christmas break, each student committed to read a particular book of the Bible prayerfully from beginning to end. One of my students, David, a young man in his mid-twenties, recounted that after Christmas his wife had gone to visit her parents in another city for several days. That left him home in their apartment with their two-year-old English beagle, Sadie. Every night around ten p.m. David would sit on the loveseat and spend half an hour on his devotional reading. Soon Sadie got the notion that this was a good opportunity to pursue her own spiritual growth, so she began hopping up and sitting next to him on the couch and putting her head in his lap. One night he got caught up in watching the news and didn't go to the loveseat at the prescribed time. Sadie came over and began to pull at his pant legs. One night he was exhausted and went to bed at 9:45 p.m. Just as he was drifting off to sleep he heard a whimpering and felt the blanket being pulled off the bed. When he looked over the side of the bed, there was Sadie, his bedspread in her teeth, there to call him to prayer. He decided that some dogs were bird dogs, and some dogs were sheepdogs, but that Sadie was a prayer dog. This parable of the Ten Virgins is a Sadie the Prayer Dog parable. It reminds us of the urgency in what seems to be an endless future.

As we live out our faith in an imperfect, troubled world, this parable can motivate us to take action in response to environmental abuse and injustice while effective action is still possible. In this parable, Matthew retains the urgency of the return of Christ in his community. While acknowledging that it is not necessarily imminent in a chronological sense, he insists that Christians have the responsibility to continue in good deeds in the extended present, in the knowledge that the time will come when they lose the opportunity for proper action. The servants in the parable of the unfaithful and faithful servants failed because they abused the time of waiting by pursuing evil deeds. The maidens in this parable fail by inactivity. They presume a gracious future without preparing for it by active discipleship. This is the definition of foolish for Matthew.

The Judgment
Matthew 25:31–46

The three parables that precede this one stress waiting for the return of Christ. This one takes listeners forward to the moment the Son of Man comes in glory (Matt. 25:31). The nations are assembled and the sheep separated from the goats (Matt. 25:32–33). This parable is similar to the Rich Man and Lazarus in that the time to repent and be converted, the time to care for the poor on one's doorstep, is past. Judgment has arrived. The king addresses each of two groups as either blessed or cursed and announces the consequences—enter into the kingdom or depart from him. He states his criterion for making these assignments—a need that they either met or did not meet: I was hungry, thirsty, a stranger, naked, sick, or in prison and you fed, gave me drink, welcomed me, clothed me, visited me."

Then the blessed ask the "when" question? "When did we see you hungry, etc., and meet your needs?" The fact that they would question their blessedness tells us something about them. Of course, those who are accursed ask the same question in verse 44, but for a different reason, to attempt to excuse themselves from their punishment. The answer to both the blessed and the accursed groups is the same. "Truly I tell you, just as you did it [or did not do it] to one of the least of these who are members of my family, you did it [or did not do it] to me" (vv. 40, 45).

The kingdom of heaven shows up where we least expect it. The presence of Jesus is hidden in the sick, the hungry, the thirsty, the naked, and the imprisoned. They are not only the "brothers" of Jesus; Jesus identifies himself with them. We recall from the Good Samaritan parable that it was the one who both saw and acted with compassion who was the neighbor to the man in the ditch. So here it is the group that both saw and met the needs of the suffering that is blessed. This is an echo of the Beatitudes in Matthew, chapter 5. There we learned that those who hunger and thirst for righteousness, who are merciful, and who are pure in heart are and will be blessed.

Paradoxically, blessedness comes from active compassion toward those whom society and, in some cases, religion, have labeled as accursed.

Earlier we discussed the three major name tags that various groups placed on Jesus to express his ministry and identity: Messiah, Son of Man, and Son of God.

Throughout his Gospel, Matthew offers a rich array of titles for Jesus. Jesus is the son of David (Matt. 1:1), the royal Messiah who was proclaimed king at his birth and whom wise men came to worship (2:1–12). He is also the Son of God, who has his origin in God (1:20), is proclaimed as God's Son at his baptism (3:17), and proves himself to be a faithful son in his confrontation with God's adversary, Satan (4:1–11). He speaks of God as his Father, and is the Son to whom the Father has delivered all things and who reveals the Father to others (11: 25–27). He is also the Son of Man, who combines qualities of servanthood and suffering with majesty and exaltation. The Son of Man has nowhere to lay his head (8:20), will suffer at the hands of those who do not recognize him (17:12), and will be betrayed into human hands and be killed before he rises on the third day (12:40; 17:22–23). The Son of Man also has authority on earth to forgive sins (9:6), is Lord of the Sabbath (12:8), is the Messiah (16:13–17), and will come to judge the earth and usher in God's kingdom (16:27–28).

This parable combines the paradoxical qualities of the Son of Man: he is the majestic, exalted Judge and King whose identity is hidden in the poor. The kingdom of God shows up where we least expect it. Will we recognize him?

Questions for Discussion

1. What reminders are there in your life that life doesn't last forever?
2. What opportunities for service are you putting off?
3. What people do you come across in your daily life that you see but don't really see?
4. Do you ever feel that others don't really see and value you? What opportunities does the kingdom of God offer you for seeing and valuing others?

7

The Reign of God Disrupts Business as Usual

Parables from Luke

The Rich Farmer
Luke 12:16–20

This parable is unique to Luke, but its spirit shows up in Jesus' teaching about treasures in heaven versus treasures on earth in Matthew 6:19–21 and in the story of the wealthy man's encounter with Jesus recounted in all three Gospels (Matt. 19:16–30; Mark 10:17–31; Luke 18:18–30). The Christian's attitude toward possessions is an important theme in Luke. In the setup to this parable, a man asks Jesus to settle his dispute with his brother over their inheritance. Jesus changes the subject from possessions to one's attitude toward them. His parable undercuts our habit of equating possessions with life. The parable shows up a rich man's inward life through a soliloquy, one of Luke's favorite ways of expressing a person's motivations and decisions (Luke 12:17–19). In several of Luke's parables the protagonist comes to a turning point (Prodigal Son, Dishonest Steward, Unjust Judge) and decides to take a different course of action. This turning point is expressed in the soliloquy. But here the rich man's words to himself express his decision to continue on his present course of accumulating more resources without sharing them. His expectation is that his comfortable life, lived without thought of the suffering of others, will continue, only better organized, with a more secure future.

There is no conversion or change of course here to propel the plot forward. In this respect, this parable is like the parable of the Rich Man and Lazarus. The man's own death, which, we are told, will happen this same evening, intervenes with appalling swiftness.

This is the only parable in Luke in which God directly addresses a character. And what God says is this: "You fool! This very night your life is being demanded of you. And the things you have prepared, whose will they be?" (12:20).

The theme of appropriate preparation for Christ's return is prominent in several other parables from the Synoptic Gospels. They include the Ten Bridesmaids, or the Closed Door (Matt. 25:1–12; Luke 13:25); the Talents (or the Entrusted Money) (Matt. 25:14–28; Luke 19:12–24); and the Great Feast (Matt. 22:1–14; Luke 14:16–24). In Luke, three other parables besides this one deal explicitly with preparation. The Rich Man and Lazarus addresses how to prepare (or not) for the reversal of fortunes to come in the next life. The Dishonest Steward and the Entrusted Money deal with how to prepare (or not) for a coming encounter with an authority figure. It is interesting that all four of these parables of preparation have money as a theme. We will discuss these others in due course, but for now it's worth asking the question "What was it about Luke's setting and audience that made this theme necessary?" Certainly it had something to do with the temptations to conformity Christian communities face in settings that value wealth and power.

The Rich Farmer parable points to the futility of devoting one's life to accumulating possessions, in light of the coming judgment. Earlier in Luke's Gospel, Jesus says, "Woe to you who are rich, for you have received your consolation" (Luke 6:24). Several questions come to mind after reading this brief parable.

For one thing, how much can one person really use or enjoy? Doesn't grain eventually rot if not used, if simply stored in silos? What is implied in the words of God to this man? "And the things you have prepared, whose will they be?" Does this imply a social reality, that the poor will get his wealth anyway, by default, so what purpose did his greed serve? Or that, no matter how carefully we plan, we can't control the dispersal of our wealth when we are no longer there to oversee it?

Even the book of Proverbs, which generally assumes that wise living will be rewarded with a degree of prosperity, is cautious about making wealth the goal of one's life. "Do not wear yourself out to get rich; be wise enough to desist. When your eyes light upon it, it is gone; for suddenly it takes wings to itself, flying like an eagle toward heaven" (Prov. 23:4–5).

The search for wisdom, living in keeping with God's will, ought to be the goal of our lives (Prov. 2:1–15). The Lord "stores up sound wisdom for the upright"(Prov. 2:7). This is a far better storehouse than silos full of more grain than one person could possibly eat in a lifetime! Wisdom is frequently equated with a wealth that is more lasting and satisfying than gold, silver, and jewels (Prov. 3:13–15). This wisdom is expressed as respect for the poor, who are, like the rich, children of God and whose advocate is God (Prov. 17:5; 22:22–23; 23:10–11).

The fool is the one who is "wise in [his] own eyes" (Prov 3:7a), who does not "fear the LORD" (3:7b), that is, does not revere God as the source of moral guidance or wisdom for daily living.

Wisdom and the wise life are equated with life, not just with longevity and prosperity, but with one's relationship with God that neither adversity nor death can take away.[1] Wisdom "is a tree of life to those who lay hold of her" (Prov. 3:18).

The realistic portion of this parable is that a rich man in Jesus' day would hoard his wealth while the poor around him were malnourished. This points to the social reality all around him. The unrealistic, or strange aspect, is that God speaks to him directly, on the futility of the priorities he has chosen in life and on the exact timing of his demise. While none of us gets the timing memo, we have the futility information. Does it make a difference in our priorities for living out the future days of our lives?

The Dishonest Steward
Luke 16:1–8a

This parable is one of the strangest of the strange. Commentators are all over the map in their opinions of what we should make of it. One scholar insists that the focus is on the radical mercy of the rich man to his steward, comparing it to the actions of the father in the parable of the Prodigal Son that precedes it. Another scholar believes that the parable illustrates the need for radical decision in light of the coming kingdom. Still another commentator sees as the focus that shrewd, dishonest preparation is better than none at all.

If we skim this parable quickly, we assume that the steward is dishonest, because of what he does in the parable, lowering the amount each debtor owed his master. If we read more carefully, we notice that the parable doesn't tell us that the steward is dishonest because of what he does in Luke 16: 5–7. It doesn't even actually come out and say that he was dishonest before that. What it does say is that charges were brought to the rich man against his manager, that he was squandering his employer's property. Was he? Or did somebody or some group want the rich man to think he was? In my view, the adjective "dishonest" refers to the actions he was accused of at the beginning of the parable, not to his actions in lowering the debtors' debts to his boss in verses 5–7. I'll explain why in a moment.

It seems as if every couple of days there is a newsmagazine show on TV about the danger of being scammed. I am to be on my guard to prevent my credit-card number from being stolen as the restaurant cashier rings up my bill. Right now, instead of writing this lesson on this parable, I ought to be standing guard next to the trash receptacle in the alley behind my house to prevent identity theft. We are so used to financial scandals that we assume the steward's actions are a first-century version of one of them. If we understand the parable's social setting, we'll see that his actions are not dishonest, just shrewd. By shrewd, I mean calculated to ensure one's own self-interest. I think this parable disrupts our usual definition of what acting in our own self-interest means. It does this in light of the reversal of fortunes the kingdom of God will bring and in light of Jesus' repeated instructions to have compassion for others.

In ancient Palestine, there was a complex social and economic relationship among landowners, stewards, peasants, and merchants. The wealthy landowners sought to get as much profit as possible from their holdings and tenants. The steward was the middleman between the landholder and the merchants and tenants in the exchange of goods and services, such as buying and selling grain, oil, and crops and collecting rents. If he was able to get an additional take for himself in these transactions, the master didn't mind; in fact, he expected it. As long as the master's profits kept rolling in and the steward did not get too conspicuous in his consumption, the master was fine with the steward's benefiting from each deal. As for the merchants and tenants, they were in a relatively powerless position, unable to directly confront the master. Their target, when they were disgruntled or felt put upon, was the steward, the master's retainer.

The steward's position in this complex social network was both privileged and vulnerable. He had a relatively high standard of living, a benefit of his being able to read and write and his training by the master, but he was completely dependent on the goodwill of the master. He himself states it in Luke 16:3: "What will I do now that my master is taking the position away from me? I am not strong enough to dig, and I am ashamed to beg." We might assume that he is whining here, selfishly unwilling to engage in honest labor. He is actually just stating the fact that he is not prepared, by physical training or by the habit of hardship, to compete with the peasant labor pool for the hardest, most menial of jobs: digging. With his strength gone, he would be reduced to begging, and in short order would die because of the malnutrition and disease that came with poverty. His situation is dire. Something must be done to prevent this future. No one can do it for him but himself.

Most commentators don't mention the fact that the parable does not directly state that the manager was squandering the rich man's property or acting dishonestly. It says that charges were brought to the master to this effect. In such a complex system of profit and self-preservation, the line between honest and dishonest was blurred, as it often is today. Parable scholar William Herzog points out that the motivation for the charges, probably from a group of tenants and merchants, may have been a desire to undermine the steward. It may be that he had contributed to their ill-feeling toward him by flaunting his higher standard of living.

The two references to "dishonesty" (16:8, 9) are probably to the charges brought against the steward at the beginning of the parable, rather than a reference to his dealings reported in verses 5–7. Those dealings, while shrewd, were not, strictly speaking, dishonest. The Torah prohibited charging interest (Exod. 22:25–27; Lev. 25:36–38; Deut. 15:7–11; 23:19–20) because it viewed it as oppressive.[2] But the wealthy found ways to charge interest under other guises. One way was to add the interest into the total amount of a debt, not in a separate line item. A contemporary analogy would be a restaurant check in which, for dining groups over a certain number of people, a gratuity is simply figured into the total, not left to the discretion of the diners.

If we are unfamiliar with the context of the parable, we assume that the steward is randomly making up percentages in verses 5–7. Actually, though, he has already done the math behind the reductions he cites to each debtor. In first-century Palestine, the more risky the commodity, the higher the interest. The interest on oil was 50 percent, because it could easily be spilled or spoil. The interest on wheat was 20 percent, because it was a more stable commodity.

While there is desperation in the steward's action, there is also premeditated, self-interested shrewdness. He calls the debtors in one by one, not giving them the chance to compare notes and collaborate against him ahead of time. He knows that his reduction of what they owe will not ensure their permanent goodwill and hospitality toward him. At best it may postpone his poverty for a short time as they invite him to a couple of meals. He may be hoping that the master cannot blame him for not extracting the interest, since to do so would be an admission that his steward, with his blessing, had been condoning charging interest, in violation of the Torah. He may be hoping his actions could make it possible for him to secure another position, as a steward for another member of the landowning elite, thereby saving him from a life of hard labor.

A better outcome still is the one that actually occurs, according to the parable. The actions of the steward please the debtors, who now owe the master less. His actions please the master, who takes pride in the shrewdness of the steward and who, besides, is now on the receiving end of goodwill from the debtors. With this proof of his shrewdness, the master can now retain him, enjoy the goodwill of his debtors, and, eventually, no doubt, find a way to recoup his temporary losses.

An understanding of the social and economic setting of the parable may clarify its inner dynamics. But does that help us understand its relevance for us? Luke, with his characteristic concern for the prudent use of money, seems to have placed after this parable a group of sayings that narrows its focus to the responsible use of wealth (16:10–13).

I'm not convinced the parable is only or specifically about the use of wealth. I think it is, more broadly, about the need to take shrewd, decisive action to prepare for the coming judgment. That action begins with a realistic assessment of our situation, the bed we have made that we are now lying in, the future that awaits us if we do not act to prevent it. It issues in a plan calculated to ensure a more positive outcome to our situation than we probably deserve.

I've said that these parables from Luke speak of a kingdom of God that disrupts business as usual. In Jesus' society, for the wealthy and those in possession of land and power, business as usual meant self-centered living focused on stockpiling material goods. For those at their mercy, it meant subsistence living as a result of unjust, top-heavy political and economic systems. Those definitions hold true today.

I think this parable commends the quality of shrewdness in a way that disrupts that pattern of business as usual. By shrewdness, I mean, actions motivated by one's astute assessment of what is in one's own best interests. This parable depicts the kingdom of God as a reality into which we enter by shrewd calculation of what is ultimately best for us and by decisive action to secure that outcome. The parable disrupts the conventional definition of what is in our best interest, as well as the patterns of action toward that goal.

The parable's commendation of shrewdness needs to be viewed in the larger context of Luke's emphases on God's mercy, Jesus' concern for the poor, and the reversal of fortunes that come with the kingdom of God. One's own best interest, in that larger context, is to act compassionately toward the poor and those who are suffering, and to refrain from making wealth the goal of one's life.

In that context, clearly it is not shrewd for someone with wealth and power to be indifferent to those who are poor or on society's margins, much less to oppress them for one's own continued gain. While such actions may be undertaken to secure one's material future, in reality such a state of living precipitates a crisis in one's condition in light of the kingdom to come. It leads to poverty and death, figuratively and literally.[3]

On the flip side, it is shrewd for one who is being taken advantage of to seek justice by opposing the unfair practices of those in power. It is shrewd for someone with resources and influence to advocate for the disadvantaged. Whatever rung we are on in the social-economic ladder, we need to take immediate, decisive, shrewd action to secure our future, and no one can take that action for us—we must do it ourselves.

Questions for Discussion

1. If you knew your life would end tonight, what priorities would you be glad you had honored? What would be your regrets?
2. How would you describe the shrewd, decisive plan you need to undertake so that your priorities are in keeping with those of the kingdom of God?

8

The Reign of God Disrupts Business as Usual

Parables from Matthew

Workers in the Vineyard
Matthew 20:1–15

The traditional interpretation of this parable sees this as a parable about the kingdom's being a kingdom based on grace rather than merit. It identifies God with the vineyard owner and equates his generosity to those hired at the eleventh hour with God's grace toward the outcast and the despised. It says, "Here is a parable of grace that is unique to Matthew's Gospel. How refreshing, since Matthew is usually all about ethical obligation and righteousness in light of a coming judgment! Finally, a departure from his usual somber, almost ominous tones." That is a pretty picture, but things may be a little more complex than that.

Some scholars feel that a shorter, simpler parable lies behind Matthew's presentation. This earlier parable encompassed Matthew 20:1–14a. Its focus was entry into the kingdom of God being based on an invitation to participate in the harvest, rather than a comparison between one's own contribution and that of others. All laborers' work is valued. Wages don't set up a hierarchy of worth in the kingdom of God. This version of the parable affirms that all workers, whenever they begin, will be honored. It affirms the worth of the outcasts and the latecomers, to whom Jesus directed his ministry.

Around this earlier parable, this theory goes, Matthew has placed a saying about judgment as a framework of interpretation. The saying is "The last will be first and the first will be last." This saying, in verse 16, follows the parable in Matthew

20:1–15). It is also, inverted, the last line of the story that Matthew places immediately before this parable (19:30), the story of the Rich Young Man, followed by Peter's question about what reward the disciples will have for being different from the Rich Young Man who cannot bear to leave behind his possessions and follow Jesus. What reward will they receive for leaving everything and following Jesus (Matt. 19:27)? Jesus assures them that "when the Son of Man is seated on the throne of his glory, you who have followed me will also sit on twelve thrones, judging the twelve tribes of Israel." He goes on to say that everyone who made sacrifices, leaving family and livelihoods for him, will inherit eternal life (Matt. 19:28–29). He concludes with the saying "But many who are first will be last, and the last will be first."

It is pretty clear that, in recounting the parable of the Workers in the Vineyard, Matthew wanted listeners to equate the latecomers with the disciples, the first hired with the Pharisees, and the vineyard owner with Jesus, the judge. In a biblical narrative, we can tell what the emphasis is by how much time and verbiage the storyteller devotes to various themes. This parable is told so that the emphasis falls not so much on the unmerited grace of the vineyard owner, as it does on the first hired workers' objection to his salary practices. The sequence of the payment, from last hired to first, is set up to provoke their public objection and his public rebuke of them, accusing them of being upset because they begrudge him his "generosity." The parable sounds a theme dear to Matthew's heart, the clear moral contrast between good and evil. It ends by pointing to the future status of the first hired as the reverse of what they think they should receive. "The first will be last" (Matt. 20:16).

If we take a traditional interpretation of the parable, we say, "Look how generous and gracious and good God is!" And look how mean-spirited and ungracious the grumbling workers are! Recent scholarship nudges us to learn something about the social setting of the parable's time, with two questions as our guide. "Is this vineyard owner really that good?" And "Are the grumbling workers really so wrong?"

Is the vineyard owner really so good? The vineyard owner was a member of the landholding elite of Palestine during the Roman occupation. Family farms had been bought up and vineyards planted on them, since higher profits came from wine than from grain. Many of those who formerly farmed their own small plots of land would have been forced into the class of day laborers, those who worked long, hard days for minimum pay. The landowner's wealth contributed to the loss of their livings.

The vineyard owner asserts that he is allowed to do what he chooses with what belongs to him (Matt. 20:15). This reflects the Romans' idea of private ownership, contradicting the Torah's insistence that God is the owner of the land. The Torah's vision was that one's blessings were given to one to share with the dispossessed in the community, not as a platform to exploit them.[1]

The denarius was a subsistence wage at the time. It was not a generous sum. His giving the unemployed men a full day's wage eased the fight for survival for them and their families only for a day.

The custom was to pay the first hired first. Why does the vineyard owner set up this elaborate scenario to humiliate them publicly? William Herzog calls this an instance of shaming the first hired. He thinks the vineyard owner is using his charity to "rob them of their sense of honor." Why does he purposely set out to provoke the negative response of those hired first and then humiliate them in front of the others?[2]

Are the grumbling workers really so wrong? They weren't so wrong if in the back of their minds was the thought, "We're poor because of your greed." Day laborers were worse off than slaves, in that landowning farmers had no stake in protecting their health. They often gave them the most dangerous jobs, and sometimes made a practice of hiring different workers every day to keep them in a weakened position. Their lack of cohesion as a group allowed the landowner in the parable to conquer them by dividing them. By speaking only to one of them, and banishing that one, he intimidates the others, putting them in their place.[3]

If the vineyard owner is not the fabulous guy we thought he was, and if the workers had a point, what do we make of the parable's bringing these two, the elite and the expendables, together? We remember that one of the affirmations about the kingdom of God we're exploring is: "The kingdom of God disrupts business as usual." What is the friction between the vineyard owner and the day laborers trying to tell us about the kingdom of God and our response to it today?

William Herzog believes the parable is meant to show us that business as usual is oppressive, and in direct contrast to the justice that is to come in God's kingdom. God is not to be equated with a member of a privileged, oppressive, capricious class of people in first-century Palestine. The vineyard owner's isolated act of generosity is no more than a whim; it doesn't amount to much, doesn't do much to alleviate suffering or improve lives or impart hope for the future. Luise Schottroff views this parable as a vignette that illuminates the plight of day laborers in Jesus' time. She sees it as an antithetical parable—God is unlike the vineyard owner: showcasing his largesse, capricious and inconsistent in his grace. So the actions of the vineyard owner are to make us think of the ways God is different from the vineyard owner, and the ways God's kingdom operates by consistent principles of justice, rather than the caprice of the privileged.[4]

The way Matthew introduces the parable ("The kingdom of heaven is like a landowner . . . ," Matt. 20:1) suggests that Matthew at least sees a positive component to the vineyard owner's behavior. We said earlier that parables contain something realistic and something strange. The realistic part is that a profit-oriented vineyard owner would calculate exactly how many laborers and how much money it would take to harvest his grapes and would hire people for only the hours he needed them, so he wouldn't have to pay a single denarius more than absolutely necessary, since anything he pays his workers is money out of his own pocket and profits. The strange part here comes when he pays those hired later as much as those hired sooner. I think we are supposed to ask ourselves, "Why on earth would he do this?" If we don't give him the benefit of the doubt, we could speculate that he wanted to make it clear to those hired first just who had the power in their relationship: the land was his; the resources were his; the decisions, which so powerfully affected their lives, were his. If we do give him the benefit of the doubt, we could speculate that he had compassion for the unemployed men who needed to work to support their families. Or perhaps he was just tired of money always being a priority over human needs and wanted to reverse it, even for a day. Maybe we are to ask ourselves, How are the actions of the vineyard owner like the kingdom of heaven? How are his repeated invitations like the kingdom of heaven? How are his equal responses to all the laborers like the kingdom of heaven? How is his disruption of business as usual like the kingdom of heaven?

I don't think the parable is about merits versus free grace. I do think it is about according equal honor to all who labor in the kingdom vineyard. The laborers who worked all day earned their wages. There is honor in that. Respect is a tribute we need to pay to the labors of others, as well as to our own. God honors our honest, godly labor. But we are not reducible to our productivity or our years of service. God invites us to harvest the kingdom because God needs our labors and because God knows we need the work. We need to participate, to receive God's gifts of strength to serve. We need to involve ourselves with others in harvesting the kingdom, in working toward justice. We do not need to compare the value of our gifts and our contributions to those of others. We do not need to begrudge God's invitation to another, or to feel that our efforts are not valuable because they are not as obvious, as dramatic, and as long-standing as those of others.

Matthew's emphasis on the first being last and the last being first is a powerful affirmation of justice and the righting of the scales in God's coming kingdom. Depending on your point of view, it is either a promise or a warning. It is a warning if you are tempted to live a self-righteous life rather than a righteous life. Matthew certainly seems to intend it as warning to the Pharisees.

It is a promise if you doubt the value of your contribution to God's kingdom, perhaps because others convey to you the message that it can't compare to theirs! Matthew seems to intend it as a promise to the disciples of the reward that will await those who sacrifice for God's kingdom.

This parable assures us that our labor is both needed and valued by God, and suggests that, in that knowledge, we can cease worrying about where we are in line and focus on our contribution to bringing in the harvest of God's kingdom.

The Two Sons
Matthew 21:28–32

In the parable of the Two Sons, another parable unique to Matthew's Gospel, the father calls one son first to go work in the vineyard. He refuses, but later relents and goes to work. The second son placates the father with a quick agreement to go and work, but he never actually goes.

Then Jesus asks, "Which of the two did the will of his father?" (Matt. 21:31). His technique is much like the one used by the prophet Nathan when he confronts King David about his adultery with Bathsheba (2 Sam. 12:1–12). He tells a story and then asks the listeners to answer a question. In choosing our reply, as listeners, we pass a judgment on ourselves.[5]

The answer seems straightforward at first glance. The first son did the father's will. But with a second glance, we see that both sons brought dishonor to the father, the first by his words, the second by his deeds. Neither son was in the right. One had the words, and the other had the deeds. We remember from Matthew's conclusion to the Sermon on the Mount that merely saying the right words does not ensure entry into the kingdom of heaven. Active obedience to Jesus' teachings must be present. In Matthew 23 Jesus warns the crowds to do as the Pharisees say, but not to imitate their actions (23:1–3).

Matthew clearly intends a tight linkage between this parable of the Two Sons in 21:28–32 and the earlier teaching about hearing and doing in 7:21 ff. In Matthew 21:30 the second son responds, "Yes, sir [*kyrie*, "sir," or "lord"]," which is the same word used in 7:21: "Not everyone who says to me, 'Lord, Lord (*kyrie, kyrie*). . . . '" The notion of Jesus' authority is also a theme that links the two passages. The teaching about the importance of following up verbal obedience with actions (7:21–23) is embodied in the parable of the Two Houses (7:24–27). The conclusion of this parable says, "Now when Jesus had finished saying these things, the crowds were astounded at his teaching, for he taught them as one having authority, and not as their scribes" (7:28–29). The parable of the Two Sons in chapter 21 is immediately preceded by Jesus' debate with religious leaders over the source of his authority for his actions and teachings.[6]

To live a life of hearing and doing the will of God is to respect and adhere to Jesus' authority as teacher and Lord. To live a life in which one gives lip service but not life service to his teachings is to disrespect the authority of Jesus.

Following Jesus' question to listeners in Matthew 21: 31, Matthew has Jesus give an explanation of the parable. It is confusing because, while the parable focuses on doing as well as saying, the explanation focuses on believing John the Baptist. The religious leaders' lack of belief in John is contrasted with the positive response of tax collectors and prostitutes to his preaching. The point is that the religious leaders who should most exemplify uprightness do not believe, while those who are thought to be unrighteous do believe and so enter God's kingdom.[7]

Matthew probably meant his community to hear this parable as a summons to the Jewish leaders of their day to imitate the first son and join them in believing in Jesus. He also meant it as a nudge to those Christians who had initially said "yes" and then wavered.[8]

Some people struggle to ever make a commitment in the first place, but once they do, are able to muster the discipline and enthusiasm to honor it. Others seem to have less trouble coming to a decision, but then have trouble following through. Many of us fall somewhere in between. To all of us imperfect disciples, Jesus addresses the question, "Which of you is doing the will of the Father?"

The "will of the Father" is a theme that occurs several times in Matthew's Gospel.

This "will" appears in Matthew's version of the Lord's Prayer, which Jesus teaches to the disciples: "Your kingdom come. Your will be done, on earth as it is in heaven" (Matt. 6:10).

Near the end of the Sermon on the Mount where, in Matthew's Gospel, the audience is the disciples, Jesus says "Not everyone who says to me, 'Lord, Lord,' will enter the kingdom of heaven, but only the one who does the will of my Father in heaven" (Matt. 7:21).

When Jesus' family comes to speak with him, Jesus makes the comment, "Whoever does the will of my Father in heaven is my brother and sister and mother" (Matt. 12:50).

When the disciples come to him with questions about who is the greatest in the kingdom of heaven, Jesus challenges their arrogance, instructing them that they will never enter the kingdom of heaven unless they become humble like a child (Matt. 18:3). Jesus tells them the parable of the Lost Sheep, concluding with this saying: "It is not the will of your Father in heaven that one of these little ones should be lost" (18:14).

When Jesus is praying in the Garden in Gethsemane, he says to God, "My Father, if this cannot pass unless I drink it, your will be done" (Matt. 26:42).

Keeping those texts in the back of our mind helps us understand just what Jesus is asking of us when he asks the question, “Which of you is doing the will of my Father?” He is asking several questions at once. Are we participating in the kingdom of God, that is, at the same time not yet here but already arrived? (Matt. 6:10.) Are we committed to active response and obedience to God and not just lip service? (Matt. 7:21.) In this way are we becoming a member of Jesus’ spiritual family? (Matt. 12:50.) Are we showing a commitment to saving the lost and the excluded? (Matt. 18:14.) Are we willing to sacrifice when necessary, on behalf of the kingdom? (Matt. 26:42.) Which of us is doing the will of God?

Questions for Discussion

1. In what ways do you fear your contributions are not as important or valued as those of others? In what ways do you judge yours to be of more value than others’?
2. How wide is the gap in your life between life service and lip service?

9

The Reign of God Disrupts Business as Usual

Parables Found in Matthew and Luke

The Feast

Matthew's Version
Matthew 22:1–14

The parable of the Feast is found in the *Gospel of Thomas* in a simpler form than it appears in either Matthew or in Luke. In the *Gospel of Thomas* version a man prepared a dinner and sent his servant to invite the guests. Each of several guests informs the servant that something has come up (a business meeting, buying a house, marriage, buying a farm), and they ask to be excused. The servant reports this to the master, who then instructs him to go out into the streets and bring back those he happens to meet so that they may dine. The closing line is "Businessmen and merchants will not enter the Places of My Father."

This brief version contains the structure that shows up in all three versions. A man prepares a feast to which guests have been invited earlier. When the servant goes out to announce that the feast is about to begin, the invited guests offer various excuses. The one giving the feast then substitutes for the invited guests people chosen at random.

The version in the *Gospel of Thomas* is similar to Luke's. Both describe a banquet, not a wedding feast as in Matthew. Thomas's closing comment about businessmen and merchants reveals his theology of rejecting worldly activity.[1]

Matthew and Luke probably received this parable from the sayings collection Q, which may have originated with an itinerant group of Jesus' followers who sought to live by his teachings and spread his message after his death. The urgency of the invitation and the theme of exclusion are thematic in Q. The parable in its earliest form may have pointed to the rejection of Jesus' message by his contemporaries and the substitution of the itinerant group that collected his sayings in the Q collection. The parable in this early form has a double focus. It conveys the vindication of Jesus' offer of forgiveness to tax collectors and sinners after the invited guests (the Jewish leaders) refused. It warns that the decisive moment has come, the feast is near, and a failure to respond will lead to exclusion from the banquet.[2]

Matthew makes this parable into an allegory. The host becomes a king and the feast becomes a feast for his son. The theme of the good and the bad (Matt. 22:10) recalls Matthew's understanding of the church as a mixed body (Matt. 13:24–27, 47–50). The parable of the Wedding Garment, which Matthew adds to the Feast parable (Matt. 22:11–14), brings in Matthew's habitual theme of discipleship against the constant backdrop of coming judgment.

Just before this parable of the Wedding Feast/Wedding Garment in Matthew we have heard two other parables: the parable of the Two Sons (Matt. 21:28–32) and the parable of the Wicked Tenants (Matt. 21:33–39). This sets up a triad of parables that all deal with rejection or refusal. The setting to which Matthew addressed his Gospel was a church that was engaged in missionary activity that was meeting with rejection. The first parable of the triad (the Two Sons) mentions the rejection of John the Baptist's ministry. The second (the Wicked Tenants) alludes to the rejection of Jesus' historical ministry. This third parable (Wedding Banquet/Wedding Garment) refers to the rejection of the preaching of Christian missionaries on behalf of the Risen Christ. The coming of God's reign is often imaged as a banquet (Isa. 25:6–8; 1 Enoch 62:14) or a wedding (Isa. 62:1–5).[3]

We flinch when we read the treatment of the man in Matthew 22:11–14. It seems so unfair that this poor man should be punished for not having the proper garment. I am reminded of the time I arrived from out of town for an ordination service and had not brought the appropriate liturgical robe for the procession. My clergy colleagues did not bind and gag me and stuff me in the closet for this infraction! What is going on with this cruel king?

It was the custom in ancient Near Eastern weddings that the guests would wear a garment that symbolized their respect for the host and the occasion. Often the host would provide a rack of such garments at the entryway for guests who had not brought theirs. Not to be wearing a wedding garment, when one could have chosen one on the way in, is a sign of disrespect for both host and occasion. The symbolism of putting on clothing reminds us of Paul's image of "putting on" as a symbol for adopting the life of discipleship to Christ (Gal. 3:27; Eph. 4:24; Col. 3:12). The wedding garment stands for the Christian life and the qualities that lead one to hear the invitation, to accept it, and to show up to honor the host.[4]

The man without the wedding garment is like the son in the prior parable who said he would come, but did not. He is a hearer but not a doer. He does not produce fruits worthy of repentance. He does not follow that higher righteousness Matthew expects of his Christian community, whether former Jews or Gentiles. In Jesus' ministry, it seems as if this parable of the Feast summoned listeners to a critical choice, to accept the authority of his teachings and to live by them. Matthew has adjusted this parable of the Wedding Banquet/Wedding Garment to address his church in its conflict with the synagogue down the street. He wants his listeners to understand that anyone who does not honor the host and the banquet, whether outside or inside his community, will not ultimately enter the kingdom of heaven.

Luke's Version
Luke 14:16–24

Luke's version of this parable is set in the context of a meal as Jesus was eating a meal on the Sabbath in the house of a leader of the Pharisees (Luke 14:1). We are told that "they were watching him closely" (Luke 14:1b).

Jesus then sees a man with dropsy and asks the lawyers and Pharisees if he should heal him on the Sabbath. They remain silent. He heals him and sends him on his way. Then Jesus teaches them to not seek the places of honor when they are invited to a wedding banquet (Luke 14:8). He follows this with instructions to invite the poor, the crippled, the lame, and the blind to their homes, rather than their friends and relatives who could easily repay them (Luke 14:12–14).

The first 14 verses of chapter 14 set up the context for Luke's version of the parable of the Feast. The focus in Luke's version of the Feast is on the inclusion of the outcasts in the banquet, a Lukan theological emphasis. The focus in Matthew's version of the parable is on the exclusion of those who rejected the invitation to the banquet. Luke contains no mention of the violent treatment of the messengers or of the punishment of the guests who refused.

Luke adds a description of the substitute guests as "the poor, the crippled, the blind, and the lame" (Luke 14: 21). Here he mentions the same four classes of guests that the believer is told to invite to his banquet in Luke 14:13 (see also Luke 7:22). In adding this fourfold description of the substitute guests, Luke emphasizes the gracious offer of the gospel to the disadvantaged that is thematic to his Gospel.

Then Luke adds a second invitation to the banquet that is not present in Matthew or the *Gospel of Thomas*—an invitation to those from the highways and hedges (Luke 14:23). Inclusiveness is an important theme for Luke. Luke was writing to a Gentile audience and may have had them in mind in stating that the servants, having scoured the thoroughfares of the town (Luke 14:21), went to the roads and lanes, presumably outside the town.[5] The host bears a striking resemblance to Jesus, whose critics said of him, "This fellow welcomes sinners and eats with them" (Luke 15:2).[6]

In the Old Testament and later Jewish literature, the final intervention of God in history to deliver his people from oppression took the form of a war against his people's enemies followed by a banquet of celebration of the Lord's victory over his enemies, the Messianic Banquet (Isa. 25:6–9; Rev. 19:9). The parable of the Feast, in the Gospels of Thomas, Matthew, and Luke, views the meal as a symbol for the kingdom of God.

So the Old Testament reference to Isaiah 25:6–9 describes a feast of celebration of victory over the Lord's enemies.[7] Deuteronomy outlines three circumstances under which someone can be excused from participating in war with Israel's enemies: building a house, planting a vineyard, and getting engaged to be married (Deut. 20:5–7). They bear a remarkable similarity to the excuses given by those who refuse to attend the Feast. Here in this parable we find that the invitation to the banquet, while it does not involve military violence, is so urgent that even excuses one might use for staying home from defending one's community are not acceptable.[8]

A marriage feast is a major occasion in village life. The excuses are without foundation, since the date would have been known for a long time, and their excuses refer to events that could have been preplanned so as not to conflict with the wedding feast. The refusals look like a group effort to shame the host. As readers, we are to wonder at the reason for this insult.[9]

Rather than accede to their effort to shame him, the host sends out servants to invite in those whom society has shamed and labeled as unclean and sinful—the poor, the ill, the disabled, and the defenseless. The final scene in Luke's version of the Feast parable depicts a messianic banquet, but not the traditional one—a grand banquet celebrating the Messiah's victory over the nation's enemies, at which anyone who is anyone is in attendance, symbolizing their inclusion in the kingdom. Rather, this is a messianic banquet whose original guests tried to shame the host by being no-shows. Their not showing up is a sign of lack of confidence in his messiahship, in his ability to conquer their enemies. The banquet hall is filled with those scorned by the religious elite of the nation as impure and sinful and unclean. They, as it turns out, are the ones who have gained entry to the kingdom of God, not by violence, not by ritual purity, but by accepting an invitation that they have interpreted, not as an annoying obligation, but as a welcome blessing.

The Talents (or the Entrusted Money)

(Parable of the Talents) Matthew 25:14–28
(Parable of the Pounds) Luke 19:12–24

The Talents (Matthew) and the Pounds (Luke) are variants of the same parable. In Luke we have a combination of two parables, much as we have in Matthew's combination of the Great Feast and the Wedding Garment. Luke, or his prior source, has introduced into the story of the Pounds a separate story about a nobleman, disliked by his countrymen, who seeks a kingdom. That story appears in vv. 12, 14, 15, and 27. The story may have a historical origin. In 4 BCE Herod the Great's son Archelaus journeyed to Rome for confirmation of his kingship over Judea (the southern part of Palestine). The Jews sent a group of fifty people to Rome to protest his appointment. He was appointed anyway, and returned to exact a bloody revenge on the people.[10] Luke's version of this parable adds this context of historical urgency to the message of the parable. There is urgency to investing your pound wisely, since destruction may come unexpectedly in an uncertain life. In Luke, the parable is placed between the story of Zacchaeus, who underwent a dramatic shift in his priorities in response to Jesus, and Jesus' triumphal entry into Jerusalem, an enacted parable of risk. Jesus' destruction in the crucifixion led to divine vindication of the way he invested his life: the resurrection.

First we'll focus on Matthew's version of the parable. By now we have noticed a couple of things about Matthew's use of parables. One is that almost all his parables end in a person or group condemned for being foolish or wicked. Most of the parables unique to Matthew (Unmerciful Servant, Vineyard Laborers, Last Judgment) end on a note of judgment. This pattern fits Matthew's polemic against Jesus' opponents and his emphasis on the need for a higher righteousness, one that involves the inner life as well as the outer.[11]

The parable of the Talents follows this same pattern. It is the third in a trio of parables: the Faithful and the Unfaithful Servant (Matt. 24:45–51; Luke 12:42–46), the Ten Bridesmaids (25:1–13), and, now, the Talents (Matt. 25:14–30; Luke 19:12–24)). These three parables have common features: In all three a powerful figure goes away for a time. In his absence people act in two contrasting ways. When he returns, he responds positively to the ones who did well, and he judges those who did not.

The first parable concerns slaves whose master is delayed. The second concerns bridesmaids when a bridegroom is delayed. This parable of the Talents concerns slaves whose master went on a journey for a long time. The first parable ends just as we would expect—the slave who was punished had gotten drunk and beaten the other slaves. The next two parables, though, feature five bridesmaids and a slave who are judged and condemned, not for acting badly, but for failing to act.

They are rebuked and punished for their passivity. Apparently this theme is important enough to be addressed, not just in one parable, but in two.[12]

The man is described as having "entrusted his property" to his slaves (Matt. 25:14). The same action is described in the parable of the Faithful and the Unfaithful Servant where the master puts a slave "in charge of all his possessions" (Matt. 24:47). This tips off the reader that the issue here will be the faithful maintenance of a trust.[13] Matthew's version of the parable of the Entrusted Money (Talents) describes a man going on a journey. He is obviously wealthy, since he can afford to travel abroad and has a staff of retainers. In Luke's parable of the Pounds, the authority figure is a nobleman who is going to a distant country to get royal power and come back. In Matthew the man gives three servants differing amounts of money, five, two, and one talent. In Luke, he gives ten servants one pound each. The amounts in Matthew are vastly more. A talent equaled about 6,000 denarii. A denarius was one day's wage, so 6,000 denarii amounted to about fifteen to twenty years' worth of wages. A pound, a *mina,* represented about 100 denarii.[14]

Matthew specifies that the man gave the servants more or less according to their ability (*dynamin*) (Matt. 25:15). "Ability" could also be rendered "power." Retainers in the households of the wealthy in ancient times gained power by the demonstration of their abilities to manage others and to increase their master's holdings and funds. So ability and power are not so different in meaning here. Some interpreters have speculated that the man is testing his staff, but it seems unlikely that he would use such massive amounts of money to test them. More likely, they have already passed numerous tests to make it into his inner circle. Testing retainers would have been done with lesser amounts of money. This is a bid by the man to enhance his resources by relying on persons with known skills, not a test for the untried.[15]

There are two diametrically opposed possible interpretations for how this parable disrupts business as usual. William Herzog and others argue that the one-talent man is the hero of the parable. He alone of the three refuses to increase his funds in the only way a retainer in a wealthy household could in those days: by extracting funds from those who were already strapped beyond bearing by both temple and Roman taxes. The wealthy elite used their wealth to make loans to peasant farmers so they could plant their crops. Interest rates were high, from 60 to as high as 200 percent. The purpose of making these loans was that the peasants would be forced to put their land up as collateral, and therefore the wealthy elite could foreclose on these loans in years when crops did not cover the incurred debt. In this way the wealthy demoted peasants from independent owners of small family plots to day laborers dependent on the owner for work. The retainers were the ones who brokered these oppressive interchanges. Though it is never said in the parable, it may be that there was an unspoken agreement that the servants would double the master's money, and as long as they did so they were free to profit themselves by some "honest graft" added on. The one-talent man, by burying his talent, refused to participate in this oppression.

In this interpretation, his accusations regarding the master's character are true (Matt. 25:24). He is not a coward, but a courageous whistleblower, willing to accept the consequences of exposing the master and the system he exploits to enhance his wealth. His master is furious, and he is ejected from his household into a future of poverty and death. In this interpretation, the parable disrupts business as usual by recommending an analogous nonparticipation in oppressive systems in contemporary life.

A second, more frequent, interpretation better fits the context in which Matthew has placed the parable, with its warning against passivity. It also makes more sense in light of the fact that the one-talent man acknowledges that his motivation was fear and timidity. In this reading, what is strange about the parable is the harsh treatment of this third servant. Rabbinic law stipulated that burying was the best safeguard against theft and that when one buries entrusted money one is free from liability for it. The one-talent man has been prudent. and he proudly presents his one talent to the returning master.[16]

The rapid and violent response of the master is shocking. The one-talent man is not guilty of drunkenness or beating fellow servants. He is only guilty of a timid prudence. In the uncertain economic world in which this parable was first told, its hearers may well have identified with the one-talent man.

He may not be without fault, however. A clue is that his characterization of the master as one who is "a harsh man, reaping where you did not sow, and gathering where you did not scatter seed" (Matt. 25:24) is never substantiated. No one but the third servant ever accuses the master of harshness in Matthew's version. The master does not accept this description of himself as accurate. It seems as if the one-talent man's accusation of harshness on the part of the master is just an excuse for his own inaction. The master points out (v. 26) that if the servant had really thought this, he would have invested his money with the bankers so he could have presented the master with interest on his return (v. 27).

On this reading, the parable still disrupts business as usual, but it does so by recommending risk rather than timid caution. Matthew places this parable as the conclusion of three parables that affirm that the return of Christ is delayed, but that it is certain. All three advise proper behavior in the interim. The time before the return of Jesus is to be used responsibly. In these parables Matthew warns against those attitudes that will bring about exclusion from God's kingdom.[17]

According to this parable, then, we are to take what ability and power we have been given and use them to increase the influence of God's kingdom on earth. God's power is different from that of a wealthy aristocrat. The parable of the Judgment, which follows the parable of the Talents, makes this clear. We do not further God's purposes by being agents of those who have more in exploiting those who have less. On the contrary, we risk seeing Jesus in the poor and the exploited; we risk pouring out our abilities and influence on their behalf.

Questions for Discussion

1. What are your excuses for not attending God's banquet? What do you think you are missing?
2. What risks have you taken for the sake of God's kingdom? What risks are you being called to take?

10

The Reign of God Is a Reign of Forgiveness and Justice

The Unforgiving Servant
Matthew 18:23–34

This parable is unique to Matthew. It is about forgiveness, but with Matthew's typical ending in which someone has to pay. A good way to get into the meaning of a parable for us is to ask ourselves: What do we wish it said instead of what it says? I would prefer a more positive version of this parable about forgiveness, one whose theme music is in a major key and that has a positive ending. My parable would go like this: A master forgives a servant's debt. The servant then goes out and sees another servant who owes him money. The second servant falls on his knees in front of the first and begs for forgiveness. Then there is a touching moment, when the first servant reaches out his hand and lifts the second servant to his feet and says something like, "Since I have just come from being forgiven by the king, how could I do anything but forgive you?" The second servant rejoices and goes and spreads the news. The news of the first servant's merciful behavior reaches the ears of the king. The first servant gets a promotion, and then there is a party. Maybe I would even have the king forgive all the debts of all his servants. But I have gotten carried away by my imaginings and forgotten where I am. I am in the Gospel of Matthew, not Luke.

All the parables unique to Matthew, except for the brief analogies of the treasure, the pearl, and the fishnet, end with someone's downfall, while the minor-key theme song of judgment plays in the background.[1] So the unforgiving servant in this parable ends up being tortured in a dungeon (Matt. 18:34). The weeds get thrown into a furnace of fire (Matt. 13:42); the laborer who dared to complain about his wages is sent packing (Matt. 20:14); the son who didn't go to the fields is eventually excluded from the kingdom (Matt. 21:32), and those who did not see Jesus in the destitute go away into eternal punishment (Matt. 25:45–46).

Now it is time for personal confession. I rolled through a red light several months ago and was stopped by a police officer and given a ticket. You will be pleased to hear that your author was very polite to the officer. I was then given the mandatory opportunity to attend "red light school" at the township building one evening a few weeks later. So there I sat with twenty or thirty of my fellow citizens now labeled "red light runners." The two-hour program began, as you would expect, with a slide show of cars destroyed by red-light runners, slides of people hurt and even killed by red-light runners, and statistics to last a lifetime. Flashing before us for a full half hour were images of the consequences of our actions. I must admit that, as weary as I sometimes get of Matthew's repeated pictures of judgment, I do scrupulously stop at yellow lights now.

Matthew must have thought that his congregation needed a warning label affixed to parables, a warning of the consequences of merely doing their religion lip service, of being hearers but not doers. A crucial expression of our obedience to Jesus' teachings is that we not judge ourselves superior to others (Matt. 7:1–5; 18:1–5) on the basis of our religious heritage or observances. The parable of the Weeds, another parable unique to Matthew among the four canonical Gospels (Matt. 13:24–30; see also *Gospel of Thomas* 57), shows us that he believed the present time is a time of grace in which God allows weeds and wheat to grow together, and it is God's prerogative to judge which is which. So we are not to judge one another, but we are to live aware of the winnowing that is to come at God's hands. The presence of forgiveness in our lives is an important criterion on which our obedience will be judged when the time comes. We are not to roll judgmentally down the road of life. Rather, we are to stop when necessary, to take stock of our own sins, and to extend the same forgiveness we have received to others. Matthew emphasizes that the one who teaches us this lesson on forgiveness is the Son of God, who has promised to be with us to the end of the age (28:20). Therefore, we are not being asked to summon this forgiveness apart from the presence of Jesus, but summon it we must.

The parable of the Unforgiving Servant is realistic and strange. It is realistic that a king would settle accounts. It is strange that he would demand that the debtor's family also be enslaved, much less sold! Jewish law stipulated that only the debtor be enslaved, not that his family be enslaved or sold. This exaggeration is meant to underscore the harshness and mercilessness of the king.

It is strange that a servant would owe such a massive amount as ten thousand talents, an amount that could never be repayable in one lifetime, since one talent was the equivalent of fifteen to twenty years of daily wages. The absurd amount highlights how tremendously grateful the first servant should be to the king for the forgiveness of such a massive debt. The monumental amount the first servant owed the king also is meant to contrast with the relatively modest amount that the second servant owes the first servant. That amount is one hundred denarii. A denarius is the equivalent of one day's wage, so this is certainly an amount that could be repaid in a timely fashion.[2]

The cruelty of the king reminds us of other violent overreactions by authority figures elsewhere in Matthew's Gospel: the king in the parable of the Wedding Garment (Matt. 22:12–13) and the master in the parable of the Talents (25:30). These sorts of reactions are missing from the parables unique to Luke.

So we have a picture here of a terribly harsh king who, inexplicably, takes pity on a servant who owes him a tremendous debt. And we have a picture of a person who has been shown tremendous mercy inexplicably unwilling to extend it to someone else.

What motivates someone who is apparently without pity to take pity?

What motivates a person who has been shown mercy to deny it to someone else?

Do we see ourselves in either of those questions? Do we need, in our lives, in our relationships, Matthew's reminder that, in light of the coming reckoning, we need to make changes in the way we do things?

The Prodigal Son
Luke 15:11–32

The parables unique to Luke, while not devoid of judgment, almost always have a more positive ending than those in Matthew. The parable of the Good Samaritan ends with the victimized man lying in an inn healing and the Good Samaritan footing the bill and promising to come back and check on him soon. The Friend at Midnight ends with the man in bed getting up to give the persistent friend a loaf of bread. The Unjust Judge ends with the judge granting the persistent widow justice. The Dishonest Steward ends with the man keeping his job and being commended for his shrewdness. The Pharisee and the Publican ends with the publican being approved by God for his humility.

Luke's parables are not without the reminder that lack of compassion has consequences. In the Rich Man and Lazarus, another parable unique to Luke, the rich man who stepped over Lazarus all those years does, after all, end up thirsty and tormented in Hades. But this cautionary picture is rounded out by the image of Lazarus, well hydrated and amply consoled at Father Abraham's side.

There are a couple of parables unique to Luke in which we are warned that, if we do not change, the outcome will not be pleasant, but we are mostly given the opportunity to change. The Rich Farmer is warned that he will die that day. Still the parable ends by God asking the farmer a question, "The things you have prepared, whose will they be?" (Luke 12:20). The reader is given a chance to fill in the blank, to answer the question. If Matthew had included this parable, he would have ended it by painting us a vivid picture of the farmer weeping and gnashing his teeth while being tortured and burning in the furnace of fire. In Luke's parable of the Barren Fig Tree, the tree still has a year to bear fruit before being cut down (Luke 13:6–9).

Luke's parable of the Prodigal Son is probably the best known and best loved of Jesus' parables. It is preceded by two brief parables that use a shepherd looking for a lost sheep and a woman searching for a lost coin as metaphors for God's saving activity. It is followed by the parable of the Dishonest Steward, in which a rich man is strangely gracious to someone of dubious reputation (and perhaps actions as well). Chapter 15, the chapter of the three "lost" parables (sheep, coin, and son), begins with the complaint of the Pharisees and the scribes that "This fellow welcomes sinners and eats with them" (15:2).

Various titles have been given to our parable, among them the Prodigal Brothers, the Foolish Father, and the Waiting Father. It falls into two parts: the first focuses on the younger son, the second on the older son. The father is the protagonist throughout the parable. The younger son asks for his share of the inheritance, probably, as the younger of two sons, a third of his father's estate (Deut. 21:17). The essence of a man's inheritance at that time was land, and the only way it could be received was on the father's death. Thus, his request was essentially, "Father, I wish you would drop dead." Even though the father could divide the land before his death, he retained rights to the use of the land. The younger son, in selling his portion, left his father without rights to the land's use.[3] A person's property was his until death, and the family's property was meant to maintain its oldest members until their death. So to demand his share early and then to dissipate it rather than to manage it responsibly for his parents' sake, is to say to his father, in effect, "You are already dead to me."[4]

He goes into the Greco-Roman world, as many Jews did to seek their fortunes in the lands around Palestine. His goal is to find himself, but he ends up by losing himself, reduced to working with unclean animals (Lev. 11:7). The parable tells us that he "came to himself" (Luke 15:17). At this point, the parable's emotional richness begins to draws us in, so that we identify with, first one, then another of its characters. The boy is hungry. He is humiliated. He knows he has made a mistake and is desperate to survive. Most of us know something of what that feels like and can feel empathy for the boy. I am a daughter. I've disappointed my parents at times in the past. It's not a good feeling.

Does this mean he genuinely repented? We can't be sure. The narrative shows him sitting among the pigs' pods, rehearsing what he will say to his father. Whether he really believes he has sinned against God and his father and is no longer worthy to be called his father's son is not entirely clear. Can we trust his sincerity? He is starving and humiliated. Is he just saying whatever it takes to fill his stomach? The story doesn't fill in this gap for us.

The culture of Palestinian villages was one of honor and shame. Honor was connected to how one was perceived in the community. Certain behaviors enhanced that honor, and certain others brought shame. The son has brought shame on his father and his whole family by his behavior. He can expect to be shamed by the village.[5]

We like to think that no one is affected by our actions except ourselves, and that we should, therefore, be able to do what we like. But the son's decision affected the whole village. It put his family's future means of making a living at risk. It undermined their honor and place in the village. In souring their relationship with their neighbors, his actions had wide-ranging effects on his family.[6]

The younger son could expect that the townspeople would conduct a *gesasah* ceremony on his return. This is not a reception in the fellowship hall, with a "Welcome Home" banner and a sheet cake. This would have been a ceremony for a son of the village who had lost his money to Gentiles or married an immoral woman. They would gather around him, breaking jars with corn and nuts, and declare that he was to be cut off from the village. His entry into the village would be humiliating as the townspeople expressed their anger and resentment toward his actions.[7]

When the father sees his son, his compassion is kindled and he moves toward him. We are reminded of the sequence in the Good Samaritan story of seeing someone suffering, having compassion, and taking action (Luke 10:33–34). He may have been seeking to protect his son from the insults of those he must pass by on the way home. His behavior is strange—fathers did not run to their children. This is more maternal behavior, as is the kiss. Here the father exposes himself to humiliation to prevent his son from being humiliated. This strange behavior is not the way the patriarchal head of a household would act in Jesus' time. But this running to meet his son is an expression of a love strong enough to make one willing to put aside one's power and position for the good of another.[8]

I'm a parent. I know what it feels like to be angry and hurt by a child and desperate to lay eyes on that child all at the same time, knowing that, if you ever do, you will give them the moon—never mind that they don't deserve it and that it may not be good for their character. As a parent, whatever struggle you are having with your child's growing pains, you cannot bear to hear a negative word about that child uttered by someone else! So I'm there with that father, running out to place himself, physically, if necessary, in between that boy and any insults that bystanders may fling at him as he makes his way home.

The father won't even let his son get through his carefully rehearsed speech before he begins issuing orders to the servants. He offers him a kiss, a sign of forgiveness (2 Sam. 14:33), a robe (a mark of distinction), a signet ring (a sign of authority), and shoes (worn only by freemen). The father throws him a banquet, rejoicing in his son's return to his father's table. He wants to point out his honored status not only to his younger son, but also to the community.[9]

The older son objects to the warm welcome and the gifts, the signs of honor. And he has a valid point. Isn't this celebrating excessive? This son of his father's (Luke 15:30) has squandered a third of the family property and now will be living off his share. He wonders if this is good parenting on his father's part. Where are the consequences? Isn't the father just enabling more irresponsible behavior on the boy's part? Where is the chore list? Where is the gradual repayment plan?

At various times in raising three children, I could have used, and still could use, some lessons in parenting from the father in this story, because his handling of the interchange with his older boy is parenting at its best. He does not condemn the older brother. He quietly assures him of his concern and love for him as well as for his younger brother. He tells him of the course of action he has chosen and leaves it up to him to decide on his own. We are left, at the end of the parable, not sure whether the older brother will go into the banquet hall or not.

Maybe the affront to his sense of fairness will overpower his yearning for the forgiveness and joy that lie within the banquet hall. Maybe he will go off to the barn and fork some hay to work off his frustrations, while the sound of the festivities annoys his ears. Or maybe his yearning for the love that lies within the banquet hall will overcome all else, and he will enter into the joy of a God who rejoices over the return of every lost child.

Questions for Discussion

1. What motivates a person who has been shown mercy to deny it to someone else?
2. What outcome do you hope for from the parable of the Prodigal Son? Where do you see yourself in the various characters?

Appendix
Parables

FROM MARK

Sower
Mark 4:3–8
Matthew 13:3b-8
Luke 8:5–8a
Thomas 9

Seed and Harvest
Mark 4:26–29
Thomas 21:4

Mustard Seed
Mark 4:30–32
Matthew 13:31–32
Luke 13:18–19
Thomas 20:1–2

Tenants
Mark 12:1–8
Matthew 21:33–39
Luke 20:9–15a
Thomas 65:1

Returning Master
Mark 13:34–36
Luke 12:35–38

FROM Q IN MATTHEW AND LUKE

House Builders
Matthew 7:24–27
Luke 6:47–49

Children in the Marketplace
Matthew 11:16–19
Luke 7:31–35

Empty House
Matthew 12:43–45
Luke 11:24–26

Leaven
Matthew 13:33
Luke 13:20
Thomas 96:1

Weather Report
Matthew 16:1–4
Luke 12:54–56

Lost Sheep
Matthew 18:12–13
Luke 15:4–6
Thomas 107

Feast
Matthew 22:1–14
Luke 14:16–24
Thomas 64

Ten Bridesmaids
Matthew 25:1–12

Talents/Pounds
Matthew 25:14–28
Luke 19:12–24

Faithful and Unfaithful Slaves
Matthew 24:45–51
Luke 12:42–46

FROM MATTHEW

Planted Weeds
Matthew 13:24–30
Thomas 57

Treasure
Matthew 13:44
Thomas 109

Pearl
Matthew 13:45–46
Thomas 76:1

Fishnet
Matthew 13:47–48
Thomas 8:1

Unmerciful Servant
Matthew 18:23–34

Vineyard Laborers
Matthew 20:1–15

Two Sons
Matthew 21:28–32

Last Judgment
Matthew 25:31–46

FROM LUKE

Good Samaritan
Luke 10:30–35

Friend at Midnight
Luke 11:5–8

Rich Farmer
Luke 12:16–20
Thomas 63:1–2

Barren Tree
Luke 13:6–9

Lost Coin
Luke 15:8–9

Prodigal Son
Luke 15:11–32

Dishonest Steward
Luke 16:1–8a

Rich Man and Lazarus
Luke 16:19–26

Undeserving Servants
Luke 17:7–10

Unjust Judge
Luke 18:2–5

Pharisee and Publican
Luke 18:10–14a

Notes

Introduction

1. See my discussion of "Assumptions Subverted by Jesus' Parables," in Alyce M. McKenzie, *Hear and Be Wise: Becoming a Preacher and Teacher of Wisdom* (Nashville: Abingdon Press, 2004), 153–59.
2. When referring to parables in their context in the Gospels, I'll sometimes include those verses before and/or after the parable that are the product of the evangelist setting it in context or giving it his own distinctive theological twist.
3. This definition is attributed to Cervantes and is quoted by James Crenshaw in *Old Testament Wisdom: An Introduction* (Atlanta: John Knox Press, 1981), 67.
4. *Treasures of the Heart,* by Daisaku Ikeda. See http://www.gakkaionline.net/Myths/Zither.html.
5. *Parables of Kierkegaard*, ed. Thomas C. Oden (Princeton, NJ: Princeton University Press, 1978).
6. Gila Safran Naveh, *Biblical Parables and Their Modern Re-Creation: From "Apples of Gold in Silver Setting" to" Imperial Messages*" (Albany: State University of New York Press, 2000), 150.
7. Bernard Brandon Scott, *Hear Then the Parable* (Minneapolis: Fortress Press, 1989), 9.
8. Harvey K. McArthur and Robert M. Johnston, *They Also Taught in Parables: Rabbinic Tales from the First Centuries of the Christian Era* (Grand Rapids: Zondervan Publishing House, 1990), 82.
9. Charles Carlston, "Proverbs, Maxims and the Historical Jesus," *Journal of Biblical Literature* 99 (March 1980): 87–105.
10. See Bruce M. Metzger, *The New Testament: Its Background, Growth, and Content,* 3rd ed. (Nashville: Abingdon Press, 2003), 113–14. Jesus' "I am" teachings include "I am the source

of living water" (John 4:14) (those who drink of the water that I will give them will never be thirsty), "I am the bread of life" (6:48), "I am the light of the world (8:12), "I am the gate" (10:9), "I am the good shepherd" (10:11), "I am the resurrection and the life" (11:25), "I am the way, and the truth, and the life" (14:6), and "I am the vine" (15:5).

11. Burton H. Throckmorton Jr., ed., *Gospel Parallels: A Comparison of the Synoptic Gospels, New Revised Standard Version,* 3rd ed. (Nashville: Thomas Nelson Publishers, 1992).
12. Metzger, *New Testament,* 96.
13. For a fuller rationale for this theory, see Metzger, 96–105. For a proposed text of Q, see Ivan Havener's *Q: The Sayings of Jesus* (Collegeville, MN: Liturgical Press, 1990).
14. See the Appendix for a listing of parables and where they appear. It clarifies which parables are unique to each Gospel, which is a clue to the aims and audience of a particular Gospel writer.
15. Metzger, p.100.

Chapter 1: The Purpose of Jesus' Parables

1. Bernard Brandon Scott, *Hear Then the Parable* (Minneapolis: Fortress Press, 1989), 14.
2. Bruce M. Metzger, *The New Testament: Its Background, Growth, and Content*, 3rd ed. (Nashville: Abingdon Press, 2003), 172.
3. Mark wants to turn down the volume on any public description of Jesus as Son of David. Matthew makes more of this motif, in his account of Jesus' birth and infancy (Matt. 1:1, 20; 2:2), Jesus' healings (9:27; 15:22; 20:30–31), and Jesus' passion (27:11, 29, 37, 42).
4. Elisabeth Schüssler Fiorenza, *In Memory of Her: A Feminist Theological Reconstruction of Christian Origins* (New York: Crossroad, 1990), 111–12.
5. Ibid., 112.
6. Ronald J. Allen and Clark M. Williamson, *Preaching the Letters without Dismissing the Law* (Louisville, KY: Westminster John Knox Press, 2006), xviii.
7. Schüssler Fiorenza, *In Memory of Her,* 121–22.
8. Ibid., 112.
9. N. T. Wright, "The Lord's Prayer as a Paradigm of Christian Prayer," *Into God's Presence: Prayer in the New Testament,* ed. Richard N. Longenecker (Grand Rapids: Wm. B. Eerdmans Publishing Co., 2001), 135.
10. Metzger, *New Testament,* 173.
11. Ibid., 174.
12. Craig L. Blomberg, *Interpreting the Parables* (Downer's Grove, IL: InterVarsity Press, 1990), 293–94.
13. Metzger, *New Testament,* 176–77.

14. Ibid., 179.
15. Ibid., 182.
16. Blomberg, *Interpreting the Parables,* 294.
17. Ibid., 294–95.

Chapter 2: The Properties of Jesus' Parables

1. A rough dating of the Synoptic Gospels places Mark at around 70 CE, Matthew at 85–90, and Luke at 90.
2. While the dating of this collection is debated, the *Gospel of Thomas* may preserve sayings that are more original than the New Testament parallels. *The Gospel of Thomas: The Hidden Sayings of Jesus* (San Francisco: HarperSanFrancisco, 1992), 13.
3. See Robert H. Stein, *An Introduction to the Parables of Jesus* (Philadelphia: Westminster Press, 1981), 55. For a fuller discussion of the role of allegory in Jesus' parables, see chapter 5, "How the Parables Are Interpreted," pp. 52–71.
4. Ibid., 55.
5. Ibid., 59.
6. C. H. Dodd, *Parables of the Kingdom*, 1935, 2nd ed., rev. (New York: Charles Scribner's Sons, 1961), 5.
7. Three authors who analyze Jesus' parables with this approach are William R. Herzog II (*Parables as Subversive Speech* [Louisville, KY: Westminster John Knox Press, 1994]), Bernard Brandon Scott (*Hear Then the Parable* [Minneapolis: Fortress Press, 1989]), and Luise Schottroff (*The Parables of Jesus* [Minneapolis: Fortress Press, 2006]).
8. For a discussion of moral and social categories in Jesus' day, see Stephen Patterson's *The God of Jesus: The Historical Jesus and the Search for Meaning* (Harrisburg, PA: Trinity Press International, 1998), 68 ff.
9. Ibid., 82.

Chapter 3: The Proclaimers of Jesus' Parables

1. Bonnie Bowman Thurston, *Preaching Mark,* Fortress Resources for Preaching (Minneapolis: Fortress Press, 2002), 3.
2. Mark 13:14 refers to "the desolating sacrilege set up where it ought not to be." This reference could be either to the statue of himself that Caligula set up in the Temple in 40 CE or to the Roman standards that flew over the Temple in 70 CE. In 70 CE the Romans destroyed the city of Jerusalem and the Temple and took its stones apart in order to recover the melted gold leaf that decorated them. Ibid., 145.
3. Stephen C. Barton, *The Spirituality of the Gospels* (Peabody, MA: Hendrickson Publishers, 1992), 41–42.
4. Ibid., 42.

5. David Buttrick, *Speaking Parables: A Homiletic Guide* (Louisville, KY: Westminster John Knox Press, 2000), 61.
6. Bruce M. Metzger, *The New Testament: Its Background, Growth, and Content,* 3rd ed. (Nashville: Abingdon Press, 2003), 177.
7. Norman Perrin, *A Modern Pilgrimage in New Testament Christology* (Philadelphia: Fortress Press, 1974), quoted in Buttrick, *Speaking Parables,* 61.
8. Ibid.
9. Howard Clark Kee, "Matthew," in *Interpreter's One-Volume Commentary on the Bible* (Nashville: Abingdon Press, 1980), 612.
10. Barton, *Spirituality,* 24.
11. Amy-Jill Levine, "Matthew," in *The Women's Bible Commentary,* ed. Carol A. Newsom and Sharon H. Ringe (Louisville, KY: Westminster/John Knox Press, 1992). For more detailed treatments of Jesus' encounters with women in Matthew's Gospel, see *A Feminist Companion to Matthew*, ed. Amy-Jill Levine with Marianne Blickenstaff (Sheffield: Sheffield Academic Press, 2001).
12. See Barton, *Spirituality,* 13.
13. The concept of Divine Wisdom embodied in a person who summons students onto the path of wise living developed in the period between the Old and New Testaments, finding expression in such Jewish books as *The Wisdom of Jesus Ben Sirach* and *The Wisdom of Solomon.* Jesus' summons to would-be followers, "Come to me, all you that are weary and are carrying heavy burdens, and I will give you rest," is found only in Matthew and bears a marked resemblance to what *The Wisdom of Jesus Ben Sirach* has Wisdom say to her followers in 6:23–31.
14. Alyce M. McKenzie, *Matthew,* Interpretation Bible Studies Series (Louisville, KY: Westminster John Knox Press, 1998), 2–5.
15. Anthony J. Saldarini, *Pharisees, Scribes, and Sadducees in Palestinian Society* (Grand Rapids: Wm. B. Eerdmans Publishing Co., 2001), 286.
16. Ibid., 283.
17. John Drane, *Introducing the Bible* (Minneapolis: Fortress Press, 2005), 396.
18. It is more accurate to say that Matthew intensifies the condemnation of Israel already present in Mark's version of the parable of the Wicked Tenants. See Mark 12:1–8; Matt. 21:33–39.
19. Barton, *Spirituality*, 73.
20. John R. Donahue, *The Gospel in Parable* (Philadelphia: Fortress Press, 1988), 127–28.
21. Jane Schaberg, "Luke," in *The Women's Bible Commentary,* 278–79.
22. Donahue, *Gospel,* 126.
23. Barton, *Spirituality,* 83.
24. Ibid., 82.
25. Ibid., 93.

26. Buttrick, *Speaking Parables*, 180.
27. Barton, *Spirituality*, 77.
28. Ibid., 82.
29. Ibid., 87–90.
30. Donahue, *Gospel*, 138.
31. Buttrick, *Speaking Parables*, 178–80.
32. Ibid., 179.

Chapter 4: The Reign of God Is Not under Your Control

1. John R. Donahue, *The Gospel in Parable* (Philadelphia: Fortress Press, 1988), 28.
2. Donahue, *Gospel*, 33.
3. Bonnie Bowman Thurston, *Preaching Mark* (Minneapolis: Fortress Press, 2002), 51.
4. Donahue, *Gospel*, 51.
5. Ibid., 37.
6. Ibid., 38.
7. Larry W. Hurtado, "Following Jesus in the Gospel of Mark—and Beyond," in *Patterns of Discipleship in the New Testament*, ed. Richard N. Longenecker (Grand Rapids: Wm. B. Eerdmans Publishing Co., 1996), 21.
8. Donahue, *Gospel*, 60.

Chapter 5: The Reign of God Shows Up where You Least Expect It (Luke)

1. Luise Schottroff, *The Parables of Jesus* (Minneapolis: Fortress Press, 2006), 132–33.
2. Ibid., 133.
3. Ibid., 134.
4. John R. Donahue, *The Gospel in Parable* (Philadelphia: Fortress Press, 1988), 169–70.
5. Donahue, *Gospel*, 171.
6. Madeleine I. Boucher, *The Parables* (Wilmington, DE: Michael Glazier, 1981), 134.
7. Donahue, *Gospel*, 187–88.
8. Schottroff, *Parables*, 7–8.

Chapter 6: The Reign of God Shows Up where You Least Expect It (Matthew)

1. Craig L. Blomberg, *Preaching the Parables: From Responsible Interpretation to Powerful Proclamation* (Grand Rapids: Baker Book House, 2004), 194.

2. Madeline Boucher, *The Parables* (Wilmington, DE: Michael Glazier, 1981), 128–29.
3. John R. Donahue, *The Gospel in Parable* (Philadelphia: Fortress Press, 1988), 103.
4. Donahue, *Gospel,* 103.
5. Donahue, *Gospel,* 104.

Chapter 7: The Reign of God Disrupts Business as Usual (Luke)

1. Alyce M. McKenzie, *Preaching Proverbs: Wisdom for the Pulpit* (Louisville, KY: Westminster John Knox Press, 1996), 31.
2. William R. Herzog II, *Parables as Subversive Speech: Jesus as Pedagogue of the Oppressed* (Louisville, KY: Westminster John Knox Press, 1994), 246.
3. I am indebted for the analysis of the social setting of the Dishonest but Shrewd Manager, to Herzog's book *Parables as Subversive Speech,* 233–58.

Chapter 8: The Reign of God Disrupts Business as Usual (Matthew)

1. Luise Schottroff, *The Parables of Jesus* (Minneapolis: Fortress Press, 2006), 210.
2. William R. Herzog II, *Parables as Subversive Speech* (Louisville, KY: Westminster John Knox Press, 1994), 91.
3. Herzog, *Parables,* 94.
4. Schottroff, *Parables of Jesus,* 216.
5. Barbara E. Reid, *Parables for Preachers: The Gospel of Matthew, Year A* (Collegeville, MN: Liturgical Press, 2001), 156.
6. Ibid., 157–58.
7. Ibid., 160.
8. Ibid., 161.

Chapter 9: The Reign of God Disrupts Business as Usual (Matthew and Luke)

1. John R. Donahue, *The Gospel in Parable* (Philadelphia: Fortress Press, 1988), 93.
2. Ibid., 94
3. Ibid., 94–95.
4. Ibid., 95.
5. Robert H. Stein, *An Introduction to the Parables of Jesus* (Philadelphia: Westminster Press, 1981), 91.
6. Ibid.

7. Bernard Brandon Scott, *Hear Then the Parable* (Minneapolis: Fortress Press, 1989), 173.
8. Donahue, *Gospel,* 141–42.
9. Scott, *Hear Then,* 171.
10. Madeleine I. Boucher, *The Parables* (Wilmington, DE: Michael Glazier, 1981), 140,
11. Paul Simpson Duke, *The Parables*, The Great Texts series, ed. John C. Holbert (Nashville: Abingdon Press, 2005), 49.
12. Ibid., 50.
13. Donahue, *Gospel,* 106.
14. Boucher, *Parables,* 139.
15. Herzog, *Parables,* 159.
16. Boucher, *Parables,* 139.
17. Donahue, *Gospel,* 109.

Chapter 10: The Reign of God Is a Reign of Forgiveness and Justice

1. Paul Simpson Duke, *The Parables,* The Great Text series, ed. John C. Holbert (Nashville: Abingdon Press, 2005), 49.
2. John R. Donahue, *The Gospel in Parables* (Philadelphia: Fortress Press, 1988), 75.
3. Brian C. Stiller, *Preaching Parables to Postmoderns* (Minneapolis: Fortress Press, 2005), 111.
4. Duke, *Parables*, 90.
5. Ibid., 92–93.
6. Stiller, *Preaching Parables,* 112.
7. Ibid., 111.
8. Ibid., 110.
9. Boucher, *Parables,* 100–101.

For Further Reading

Barton, Stephen C. *The Spirituality of the Gospels.* Peabody, MA: Hendrickson Publishers, 1992.

Boucher, Madeleine I. *The Parables.* Wilmington, DE: Michael Glazier, 1981.

Donahue, John R. *The Gospel in Parable.* Philadelphia: Fortress Press, 1988.

Griffith-Jones, Robin. *The Four Witnesses: The Rebel, The Rabbi, The Chronicler, and the Mystic.* San Francisco: HarperSanFrancisco, 2000.

McKenzie, Alyce M. *Matthew.* Interpretation Bible Study Series. Louisville, KY: Westminster John Knox Press, 1998.

Metzger, Bruce M. *The New Testament: Its Background, Growth, and Content.* 3rd ed. Nashville: Abingdon Press, 2003.

Newsom, Carol A., and Sharon H. Ringe, eds. *The Women's Bible Commentary.* Louisville, KY: Westminster/John Knox Press, 1992.

Patterson, Stephen J. *The God of Jesus: The Historical Jesus and the Search for Meaning.* Harrisburg, PA: Trinity Press International, 1998.

Reid, Barbara E. *Parables for Preachers: The Gospel of Matthew, Year A.* Collegeville, MN: Liturgical Press, 2001.

Schottroff, Luise. *The Parables of Jesus.* Minneapolis: Fortress Press, 2006.

Thurston, Bonnie Bowman. *Preaching Mark.* Fortress Resources for Preaching. Minneapolis: Fortress Press, 2002.